ISAIAH FOR TODAY

Mark E. Petersen

ISAIAH FOR TODAY

Deseret Book Company
Salt Lake City, Utah
1981

© 1981 Deseret Book Company
All rights reserved
Printed in the United States of America
First printing September 1981
Second printing April 1982
Library of Congress Cataloging in Publication Data

Petersen, Mark E.
  Isaiah for today.

  Includes index.
  1. Bible. O.T. Isaiah—Criticism, interpretation,
etc. 2. Mormon Church—Doctrinal and controversial works.
I. Title.
BS1515.2.P47   224'.106   81-12476
ISBN 0-87747-882-1   AACR2

CONTENTS

1   Isaiah Saw Our Day   1
2   Backward or Forward?   5
3   Who Was Isaiah?   9
4   Jerusalem's Defense   13
5   Sennacherib's Methods   17
6   Assyrian Persuasion   20
7   Hezekiah's Illness   23
8   Isaiah Saw God!   26
9   He Testified of Christ   30
10   Predictions of Christ   34
11   Isaiah and Abinadi   41
12   ''Wonderful, Counseller''   45
13   Hope for the Dead   48
14   Isaiah's Second Chapter   54
15   What Isaiah Saw   61
16   Templc Hill   66
17   Our Hymn of Praise   71
18   Why Build Temples?   73
19   The Marvelous Work   77
20   Nephi's Explanation   82
21   The Unlearned Man   87
22   ''One That Is Learned''   92
23   Only by Divine Power   98
24   Destroyed Suddenly   102
25   ''We Have Got a Bible . . .''   109
26   Ezekiel's Sticks   114
27   Jesus and Isaiah   120
28   Teachings of Jesus   126
29   Scattered Israel   132

30   The Old Jerusalem   135
31   Who Wrote Isaiah?   140
32   Isaiah as a Poet   143
33   What Isaiah Taught   150
34   Isaiah and Lucifer   154
35   His Voice to Us   159
      Index   161

Trust ye in the Lord for ever:
For in the Lord Jehovah is
Everlasting strength.
            —Isaiah 26:4

He shall feed his flock like a
Shepherd: he shall gather the
Lambs with his arm, and
Carry them in his bosom, and
Shall gently lead those
That are with young.
            —Isaiah 40:11

Chapter One

ISAIAH SAW
OUR DAY

More than any other biblical writer, Isaiah is a prophet for today.

As one of scripture's most penetrating voices affirming the divinity of the Savior and heralding his ministry, this Hebrew prophet opens before our eyes the panorama of God's dealings with man in times past, in the present when we ourselves live, and in days to come.

"Great are the words of Isaiah," the Savior declared. (3 Nephi 23:1.) And great is his message to the Latter-day Saints.

He gazed on our day and prophesied concerning it. He saw the restoration of the gospel and the work of the Prophet Joseph Smith.

He foresaw the coming forth of the Book of Mormon as a marvelous work and a wonder, and observed its miraculous effect upon an unbelieving world. Even the blind would read its inspired pages, the deaf would hear its words, and "the poor among men shall rejoice in the Holy One of Israel." (Isaiah 29:19.)

He envisioned the Saints in the tops of the mountains and their temple established above the hills. It was the house of the Lord, and all nations flowed unto it.

He saw two capital cities at the opening of the Millennium, Zion in America from which will go the divine law, and the Old Jerusalem—renewed—from which will issue the sacred word of God.

He revealed that the Lord will there "teach us of his ways, and we will walk in his paths" (Isaiah 2:3), and the peace of heaven will descend upon the earth.

But above all else, Isaiah bore a mighty testimony of

Christ in a voice that comes down through the centuries to this day when atheism spreads rapidly in the earth, and when strong delusions take men's minds away from the Savior into paths of distress and error.

Isaiah's testimony of Christ, if carefully read now, prepares the faithful against the time when men's hearts shall fail them. He braces us for this present day when intellectualism scoffs at the virgin birth, denies the divine creation, and ridicules the sacred revelation that man is a child of God and may become like him.

Such critics do not fear God, for they do not so much as believe that he exists.

Isaiah foresaw that the Savior would be born of Mary. He described the ministry of Jesus in Palestine, and portrayed the Lord's great humility, his rejection by the world, his death in the midst of the wicked, and his burial with the rich.

He saw also this humble Christ as God Almighty who will return in a glorious second coming to gather his sheep as a shepherd, reassemble the tribes of Israel, establish Zion, and begin his millennial reign.

He saw that the Lord will come to judgment, destroy wickedness, and enthrone the righteous Saints to live and reign with him for a thousand years.

He saw the people and said that they ''draw near me with their mouth, and with their lips do honour me, but have removed their heart far from me, and their fear toward me is taught by the precept of men;

''Therefore, behold, I will proceed to do a marvellous work among this people, even a marvellous work and a wonder: for the wisdom of their wise men shall perish, and the understanding of their prudent men shall be hid.'' (Isaiah 29:13-14.)

And did he tell us when this shall be? He did! That is now! His prophecies are for today!

Moroni saw this also and wrote to us as he neared his own death: ''Search the prophecies of Isaiah.'' (Mormon 8:23.)

Jesus gave us this commandment as he visited the Nephites: "Behold, I say unto you, that ye ought to search these things. Yea, a commandment I give unto you that ye search these things diligently; for great are the words of Isaiah." (3 Nephi 23:1.)

This prophet, Isaiah, spoke in clear and frightening terms to the people of his day and warned them against the destruction that threatened them. But they disregarded him.

He spoke just as vigorously both *of* us and *to* us of today. He saw that we too live in a time of apostasy, even as did the people of his time. He saw the tribulations of the last days.

Looking toward them he said, "The earth mourneth and fadeth away, the world languisheth and fadeth away, the haughty people of the earth do languish. The earth also is defiled under the inhabitants thereof; because they have transgressed the laws, changed the ordinance, broken the everlasting covenant." (Isaiah 24:4-5.)

And then he followed with this frightful prediction: "Therefore hath the curse devoured the earth, and they that dwell therein are desolate: therefore the inhabitants of the earth are burned, and few men left." (Isaiah 24:6.) He saw the Lord come to judgment!

Isaiah said even further as he looked to the day in which we live: "And it shall be, as with the people, so with the priest; as with the servant, so with his master; as with the maid, so with her mistress; as with the buyer, so with the seller; as with the lender, so with the borrower; as with the taker of usury, so with the giver of usury to him. The land shall be utterly emptied and utterly spoiled: for the Lord hath spoken his word." (Isaiah 24:2-3.)

"Behold, the Lord maketh the earth empty, and maketh it waste, and turneth it upside down, and scattereth abroad the inhabitants thereof." (Isaiah 24:1.) So fearful will be his judgment.

In that day also, "the earth shall reel to and fro like a

drunkard, and shall be removed like a cottage; and the transgression thereof shall be heavy upon it; and it shall fall, and not rise again. . . . Then the moon shall be confounded, and the sun ashamed" as a sign preliminary to his coming. (Isaiah 24:20, 23.)

Great destruction is projected for the wicked in these last days, but for the righteous there will be a joyful reward. In their midst the Lord of hosts "shall reign in Mount Zion and in Jerusalem" (both in America and Palestine), and his reign shall be glorious. (Isaiah 24:23.)

Chapter Two

BACKWARD OR FORWARD?

Only the Latter-day Saints truly understand Isaiah. The Book of Mormon indicates that one must know "concerning the manner of prophesying among the Jews" to comprehend his teachings.

We read: "Now I, Nephi, do speak somewhat concerning the words which I have written, which have been spoken by the mouth of Isaiah. For behold, Isaiah spake many things which were hard for many of my people to understand; for they know not concerning the manner of prophesying among the Jews." (2 Nephi 25:1.)

The reason Nephi's brothers did not understand the meaning of Isaiah's words is that Nephi had "not taught them many things concerning the manner of the Jews." He explained that he did not so instruct his brothers because of their own "doings of abominations" and "works of darkness." (2 Nephi 25:2.)

But Nephi understood Isaiah, quoted generously from him in his writings on the plates that later were included in the Book of Mormon, and thus provided for us an understanding of much of what Isaiah said.

The teachings of Book of Mormon prophets, and especially the instruction of the Savior as he ministered among the Nephites, open to Latter-day Saints a comprehension of Isaiah that is far beyond the scope of any part of the sectarian world. It greatly exceeds the understanding of the Jews themselves, because like the Christians, they are blind to the work of the Lord in these latter days whereby the gospel was restored. They are utterly unaware of the mission of Christ, both in the meridian of time and in the latter days.

Much of Isaiah's work points to the Savior, Jesus of Nazareth, who died on the cross. It has to do with his second coming also, and the preparation being provided by The Church of Jesus Christ of Latter-day Saints for that glorious event.

To understand Isaiah, people need to understand the Latter-day Saint point of view. They cannot and never will understand him otherwise. Both Jews and Christians alike grope in darkness concerning this matter until they are willing to accept the restoration of the gospel through the Prophet Joseph Smith.

A large part of Isaiah's writings, of course, have to do with the time in which he lived. But for us that is all past. That is history. We of today need to study those portions of Isaiah which relate to the twentieth century, even looking forward to the twenty-first century, now not far away.

When the Savior commands us to read Isaiah, we should respond. But to understand it, we must read the Book of Mormon along with it, for that volume opens our eyes to the genuine meaning in his words. And further, we must look to the teachings of the Prophet Joseph Smith, who also provides valuable background for those ancient prophecies.

It is sad indeed to read the efforts of both Jewish and Gentile scholars as they try to interpret some of Isaiah's words. Note this concerning one of the passages most dear to us: "Therefore the Lord himself shall give you a sign; Behold, a virgin shall conceive, and bear a son, and shall call his name Immanuel." (Isaiah 7:14.)

Following is a typical example of secular understanding: "This very year . . . a young woman will have a son and call his name Immanuel. . . . Before the boy shall be two or three years old, the allied kings will have departed from Judah. Then evil days will come upon Judah, such as she has not seen since the secession of Ephraim. Egypt and Assyria will lay the land waste." (Margolis and Marx, *A History of the Jewish People,* Jewish Publication Society of America, 1927, p. 97.) There is no mention of the true Immanuel, the Messiah.

The passage in Isaiah 2:1-5 we interpret as relating to the coming of the Saints to Salt Lake Valley and the building of their modern Zion there, together with a temple. It is interpreted by the Jews, of course, to relate only to their Jerusalem. They translate the scripture in this way, however, although they associate it with Palestine:

"In the days to come the Mount of the Lord's House shall stand firm above the mountains, and tower above the hills; and all the nations shall gaze on it with joy.

"And the many peoples shall go and shall say: 'Come, Let us go to the mount of The Lord, to the House of the God of Jacob, That he may direct us according to his ways, And that we may walk in his paths,' For direction shall be forthcoming from Zion, And words of the Lord from Jerusalem.

"Thus he will judge among the nations and arbitrate for the many peoples, And they shall beat their swords into plowtips and their spears into pruning hooks: Nation shall not take up Sword against nation; They shall never again know war." (*Encyclopedia Judaica,* New York: Macmillan, 9:51.)

Their translated version of this scripture is most interesting and further sustains the Latter-day Saint point of view. But the true meaning is entirely lost on both Jews and Christians. Which of any of the sectarian groups recognizes the facts in the case?

Similarly, the predictions of Isaiah with respect to the coming forth of the Book of Mormon (Isaiah 29) have no true meaning at all to either Jew or Gentile. How could they know? They do not have the key to prophecy, and they are blinded by the teachings of men.

Only because of the Prophet Joseph Smith do we understand chapter 29 of Isaiah.

And who of the Jews or Gentiles understands the first verse in Isaiah 61? It is quoted by the Savior himself in

Luke 4:18-19, but who understood it even in the Lord's day?

Was salvation for the dead—was the Savior's preaching to the departed spirits—ever in the minds of any Christian denomination? Did the Jews believe in such vicarious work? Did it not take the restoration of the gospel to make this passage clear?

And consider chapter 53 of Isaiah. Which Jew, orthodox or not, relates this to Jesus of Nazareth, plain as the scripture is? Most Christians accept it, but even now many of them are beginning to reject Christ as the Son of God; they no longer believe in his atonement, which is what chapter 53 is all about.

A true knowledge of that scripture comes only in the light of modern revelation through the Prophet Joseph Smith and through the Book of Mormon.

Isaiah is definitely for today. His dealings with the ancient kings of Judah and his confrontations with them over the attacks of the Assyrians and the Babylonians are all in the past. Reference to them is strictly historical and has little relevance for us.

But his writings concerning Christ, the restoration of the gospel, the gathering of the Twelve Tribes, and the second coming of the Lord are all relevant—very much so. In them he writes both *about* us and *to* us who live right now. He not only tells much about the restoration of the gospel that has already taken place, such as the coming forth of the Book of Mormon, but he also foretells the signs of the coming of Christ. The signs of the times are now all about us. Shall we not give heed to them?

Chapter Three

WHO WAS ISAIAH?

Both Jewish and Christian scholars debate the question: Who was Isaiah?

They have a variety of answers, including the theory that there may have been two or three authors of various sections of that work. But despite their differences on this point, all agree that this book is one of the greatest in the Bible.

One Jewish writer declares Isaiah to be "the greatest of the Hebrew prophets of whom literary monuments remain." (*The Jewish Encyclopedia,* New York and London: Funk and Wagnalls, 1904, 6:635.)

Isaiah was a seer, a prophet, and a revelator. He was privileged to see God, "sitting upon a throne, high and lifted up." (Isaiah 6:1.) At this glorious sight the prophet was greatly humbled, and wrote: "Woe is me! for I am undone; because I am a man of unclean lips, and I dwell in the midst of a people of unclean lips: for mine eyes have seen the King, the Lord of hosts." (Isaiah 6:5.)

Isaiah was a keen political observer of his times, and he constantly counseled his country's rulers, even when they resented it. He lived to be eighty years old and then died a martyr at the hands of a cruel and jealous king.

His own book says that he was the son of Amoz and that he lived in Jerusalem. According to the Babylonian Talmud, Amoz was a brother of Amaziah, king of Judah. Isaiah was contemporary with the prophet Micah and lived slightly after Hosea and Amos. He labored in Judah, which had been divided from the northern kingdom, or Ephraim. Hosea and Amos ministered in the north. Isaiah labored primarily within the city of

Jerusalem, while the record indicates that Micah served mostly in the rural areas. The kings under whom Isaiah lived were Uzziah, who died in the year that Isaiah "saw the Lord"; Jothan; Ahaz; Hezekiah; and Manesseh, by whom he was martyred.

Isaiah is mentioned outside of his own book in 2 Kings 19 and 20 and in 2 Chronicles 26 and 32.

Isaiah 8 indicates that he was married, as were all good Jewish men, and that he had children, mentioned in both chapters seven and eight. His wife is spoken of as a "prophetess." The *Jewish Encyclopedia* (6:636) says further: "By her solidarity [speaking of his wife] with her husband she is detached from the unholy people among whom she dwells, and made, as it were, sacrosanct. His children, too, are 'signs and omens' of divine appointment, and one may conjecture that if Isaiah ever pictured the worst disaster coming to Jerusalem, he saw himself and his family, like Lot of old, departing in safety (for some work reserved for them by God) from the doomed city."

We read further that "according to the Rabbis, Isaiah was a descendant of Judah and Tamar," and that his father, Amoz, was himself a prophet and a brother of King Amaziah. In measuring the stature of Isaiah, this authority continues: "In the order of greatness Isaiah is placed immediately after Moses by the Rabbis; in some respects Isaiah surpasses even Moses."

Although he was friendly with some of the Jewish kings, and greatly assisted them through his inspired advice, Isaiah also suffered the enmity of Manasseh, who brought about his death.

The prophet in his old age is said to have been "sawn asunder" by Manasseh. Various versions of his death appear, including that which is found in the Babylonian Talmud, which quotes a genealogical record in Jerusalem to the effect that the prophet was "swallowed by a cedar tree." When King Manasseh learned of it, he ordered the tree sawed in half with Isaiah inside it.

Another version says that Isaiah fled from the king's wrath and found refuge in a hollow tree. When his pursuers searched for him, they discovered a portion of his garment hanging outside the tree. This they reported to the king, who ordered them to saw the tree in half as it stood there. In the process, Isaiah suffered the same fate as the tree.

Some commentators think that the apostle Paul referred to this event when he wrote: "And others had trial of cruel mockings and scourgings, yea, moreover of bonds and imprisonment: They were stoned, they were *sawn asunder,* were tempted, were slain with the sword: they wandered about in sheepskins and goatskins; being destitute, afflicted, tormented." Of those who thus were afflicted for the Lord's sake, Paul further says: "(Of whom the world was not worthy:) they wandered in deserts, and in mountains, and in dens and caves of the earth," all of this indicating how severely the faithful were persecuted. (Hebrews 11:36-38.)

Still another version of the prophet's death is related in the Jewish Talmud. Of it Funk and Wagnalls says:

> It is related in the Talmud that Rabbi Simeon ben 'Azzai found in Jerusalem an account wherein it was written that Manasseh killed Isaiah.
> Manasseh said to Isaiah, "Moses, thy master, said, 'There shall no man see God and live' (Ex. xxxiii. 20, Hebr.); but thou hast said, 'I saw the Lord seated upon his throne' " (Isa. vi. 1, Hebr.); and went on to point out other contradictions—as between Deut. iv. 7 and Isa. lv. 6; between Ex. xxxiii. 26 and II Kings xx. 6.
> Isaiah thought: "I know that he will not accept my explanations; why should I increase his guilt?" He then uttered the Unpronounceable Name, a cedar-tree opened, and Isaiah disappeared within it.
> Then Manasseh ordered the cedar to be sawn asunder, and when the saw reached his mouth Isaiah died; thus was he punished for having said, "I dwell in the midst of a people of unclean lips" (Yeb. 49b).
> A somewhat different version of this legend is given in the Yerushalmi (Sanhedrin x.). According to that version Isaiah, fearing Manasseh, hid himself in a cedar-tree, but his presence was betrayed by the fringes of his garment, and Manasseh caused the tree to be sawn in half.

A passage of the Targum to Isaiah quoted by Jolowicz ("Die Himmelfahrt und Vision des Prophets Jesajas," p. 8) states that when Isaiah fled from his pursuers and took refuge in the tree, and the tree was sawn in half, the prophet's blood spurted forth.

From Talmudical circles the legend of Isaiah's martyrdom was transmitted to the Arabs ("Ta' rikh," ed. De Goeje, i. 644). (*Jewish Encyclopedia* 6:636.)

Chapter Four

JERUSALEM'S DEFENSE

Isaiah was probably the greatest patriot in the nation of Judah in his time. He was mighty both in inspired advice to the kings and in actual prophecy as he sought to preserve his nation from repeated invasions by its enemies.

At first it was Syria and the northern kingdom of Israel that threatened Judah. Later Assyria turned from being a friend and defender to a plundering enemy.

As the threat of invasion by Syria and Israel became imminent, Isaiah went to the wicked King Ahaz and pleaded earnestly with him to turn to God for his defense. But being without any faith in Jehovah, Ahaz disregarded him completely. He depended more on an alliance with Assyria than he did on any divine aid, either from Jehovah or from his pagan deities.

From the time of Jehoram, son of Jehoshaphat, the Kingdom of Judah had lapsed deeply into idolatry, influenced and encouraged by Athaliah, the daughter of the apostate King Ahab and his devilish wife Jezebel. Ahaz reached such depths in his idolatry that he even sacrificed his own son on the heathen altar.

When the kings of Syria and Ephraim, or Israel, as the northern nation was called, conspired against Judah, Isaiah again warned Ahaz to turn to God for his protection. Ahaz, however, appealed to Tiglath-pileser, king of Assyria, for assistance, and as an inducement he turned over to that monarch the treasures of both the temple and the palace.

The Assyrians went against Syria and Ephraim, or Israel, as Ahaz had asked, and in the battles that followed, both Rezin, king of Syria, and Pekah, king of Israel, were killed.

At this point Ahaz went to Damascus, which was taken in the war, and there saw a huge pagan altar, which he promptly duplicated in the city of Jerusalem. Against this idolatrous act, Isaiah raised his powerful voice. But still the king paid no heed, and paganism spread even further among the Jews. By the time Ahaz died, the kingdom had reached a new low in apostasy.

Isaiah again prophesied the destruction of the kingdom and the enslavement of the whole nation if they failed to repent.

Following the death of Ahaz, his son Hezekiah became king. He came to the throne when he was twenty-five years of age and reigned for twenty-nine years.

A righteous man, Hezekiah accepted the worship of Jehovah and moved at once to eradicate idolatry from the land. After repairing the temple, he restored temple worship and reorganized the work of the priests and Levites. He thoroughly cleansed the temple of every vestige of pagan worship and again resumed the sacred sacrifices prescribed by Moses. He also cleansed the land of the "high places" where the pagan gods had been worshipped under Ahaz, and sent messengers to all Israel, in both north and south kingdoms, to join in his reinstituted celebration of the Passover.

The northern kingdom scorned the invitation and abused the messengers. But Hezekiah proceeded regardless, and the scripture indicates that through this observance there was greater joy in Judah than at any time since the days of Solomon. Hezekiah successfully defended Judah against the Philistines and retook all of the cities which his father had lost.

In all his righteous efforts, including his military undertakings to restore and preserve the kingdom, Hezekiah had as his constant ally and adviser the prophet Isaiah.

Since his father, Ahaz, had become indebted to Assyria, that nation continued to demand a heavy tribute from Judah in payment of their part in the war with Syria and Ephraim. This was painful for the people of Judah to bear, and Hezekiah sought means to escape this burden.

The king's political advisers urged him to seek an alliance with Egypt and then begin a revolt against Assyria. Isaiah regarded such a proposal as a sign of defection from God. As he had told Ahaz previously, now he urged Hezekiah to depend on the Lord, who would protect them if they would but serve Him.

Hezekiah did rebel against Assyria. In the fourth year of his reign, Shalmaneser invaded nearby Samaria but did not come into Judah. However, in the fourteenth year of his reign, Jerusalem was attacked by Sennacherib, son of Sargon, who ascended his father's throne after Sargon was slain in 705 B.C. This monarch not only invaded Judah's capital city, but, according to the historical records, his armies also captured forty-six other towns and carried away two hundred thousand captives. (See 2 Kings 18; 2 Chronicles 28-30.)

The Assyrians were fierce and heartless invaders. When they had formerly seized Babylon, they had virtually massacred the populace there. It was they who took Nineveh, where they built a tremendous palace, now the envy of archaeologists. It was fifteen hundred feet long and seven hundred feet wide. They also brought water into the city by means of a system of canals, evidence of which still remains.

Funk and Wagnall's *Jewish Encyclopedia* (6:380) has this interesting thing to say about the invasion of Judah:

There is . . . an essential difference between II Kings, on the one hand, and Isaiah and II Chron., on the other, as to the invasion of Sennacherib. According to the former, Sennacherib first invaded Judah in the fourteenth year of Hezekiah, and took all the fortified cities (the annals of Sennacherib report forty-six cities and 200,000 prisoners).

Hezekiah acknowledged this fault and parleyed with Sennacherib about a treaty. Sennacherib imposed upon Hezekiah a tribute of three hundred talents of silver and thirty talents of gold; and in order to pay it Hezekiah was obliged to take all the silver in the Temple and in his own treasuries, and even to "cut off the gold from the doors of the Temple" (II Kings xviii. 13-16). Sennacherib, however, acted treacherously. After receiving the gold and the silver he sent a large army under three of his officers to beseige Jerusalem, while he himself with the remainder of his troops remained at Lachish (*ib*. xviii. 17).

The contrary is related in II Chronicles. After Sennacherib had invaded Judah and marched toward Jerusalem, Hezekiah decided to defend his capital. He accordingly stopped up the wells; diverted the watercourse of Gihon, conducting it to the city by a subterranean canal (II Chron. xxxii. 30; Ecclus. [Sirach] xlviii. 17); strengthened the walls; and employed all possible means to make the city impregnable (II Chron. xxxii. 1-8).

Still the people of Jerusalem were terror-stricken, and many of Hezekiah's ministers looked toward Egypt for help. Isaiah violently denounced the proceedings of the people, and derided their activity in fortifying the city (Isa. xxii. 1-14).

The account from the arrival of Sennacherib's army before Jerusalem under Rabshakeh till its destruction is identical in II Kings, Isaiah, and II Chronicles. Rabshakeh summoned Hezekiah to surrender, derided his hope of help from Egypt, and endeavored to inspire the people with distrust of Hezekiah's reliance on providential aid. But Sennacherib, having heard that Tirhakah, King of Ethiopia, had marched against him, withdrew his army from Jerusalem. He sent messages to Hezekiah informing him that his departure was only temporary and that he was sure of ultimately conquering Jerusalem. Hezekiah spread open the letters before God and prayed for the delivery of Jerusalem.

Isaiah prophesied that Sennacherib would not again attack Jerusalem; and it came to pass that the whole army of the Assyrians was destroyed in one night by "the angel of the Lord" (II Kings xviii. 17-xix.; Isa. xxxvi.-xxxvii.; II Chron. xxxii. 9-22).

Chapter Five

SENNACHERIB'S METHODS

Sennacherib, a mighty man of war, was the terror of many lands. He used every means of attack on Judah, including much verbal persuasion and threats of military action. With Isaiah's help, however, Hezekiah held firm in the faith, and so encouraged his people.

"And when Hezekiah saw that Sennacherib was come, and that he was purposed to fight against Jerusalem, He took counsel with his princes and his mighty men to stop the waters of the fountains which were without the city: and they did help him.

"So there was gathered much people together, who stopped all the fountains, and the brook that ran through the midst of the land, saying, Why should the kings of Assyria come, and find much water?

"Also he strengthened himself, and built up all the wall that was broken, and raised it up to the towers, and another wall without, and repaired Millo in the city of David, and made darts and shields in abundance.

"And he set captains of war over the people, and gathered them together to him in the street of the gate of the city, and spake comfortably to them, saying, Be strong and courageous, be not afraid nor dismayed for the king of Assyria, nor for all the multitude that is with him: for there be more with us than with him: With him is an arm of flesh; but with us is the Lord our God to help us, and to fight our battles. And the people rested themselves upon the words of Hezekiah king of Judah.

"After this did Sennacherib king of Assyria send his servants to Jerusalem, (but he himself laid siege against Lachish, and all his power with him,) unto Hezekiah king of Judah, and unto all Judah that were at Jerusalem, saying,

"Thus saith Sennacherib king of Assyria, Whereon do ye trust, that ye abide in the siege in Jerusalem?

"Doth not Hezekiah persuade you to give over yourselves to die by famine and by thirst, saying, The Lord our God shall deliver us out of the hand of the king of Assyria?

"Hath not the same Hezekiah taken away his high places and his altars, and commanded Judah and Jerusalem, saying, Ye shall worship before one altar, and burn incense upon it?

"Know ye not what I and my fathers have done unto all the people of other lands? were the gods of the nations of those lands any ways able to deliver their lands out of mine hand?

"Who was there among all the gods of those nations that my fathers utterly destroyed, that could deliver his people out of mine hand, that your God should be able to deliver you out of mine hand?

"Now therefore let not Hezekiah deceive you, nor persuade you on this manner, neither yet believe him: for no god of any nation or kingdom was able to deliver his people out of mine hand, and out of the hand of my fathers: how much less shall your God deliver you out of mine hand?

"And his servants spake yet more against the Lord God, and against his servant Hezekiah.

"He wrote also letters to rail on the Lord God of Israel, and to speak against him, saying, As the gods of the nations of other lands have not delivered their people out of mine hand, so shall not the God of Hezekiah deliver his people out of mine hand.

"Then they cried with a loud voice in the Jews' speech unto the people of Jerusalem that were on the wall, to affright them, and to trouble them; that they might take the city. And they spake against the God of Jerusalem, as against the gods of the people of the earth, which were the work of the hands of man.

"And for this cause Hezekiah the king, and the prophet Isaiah the son of Amoz, prayed and cried to heaven.

"And the Lord sent an angel, which cut off all the mighty men of valour, and the leaders and captains in the camp of the king of Assyria. So he returned with shame of face to his own land. And when he was come into the house of his god, they that came forth of his own bowels slew him there with the sword.

"Thus the Lord saved Hezekiah and the inhabitants of Jerusalem from the hand of Sennacherib the king of Assyria, and from the hand of all other, and guided them on every side. And many brought gifts unto the Lord of Jerusalem, and presents to Hezekiah king of Judah: so that he was magnified in the sight of all nations from thenceforth." (2 Chronicles 32:2-23.)

Chapter Six

ASSYRIAN PERSUASION

The devious methods of the Assyrians were exposed by Isaiah as he records the defense made against them by Judah.

"Now it came to pass in the fourteenth year of king Hezekiah, that Sennacherib king of Assyria came up against all the defenced cities of Judah, and took them.

"And the king of Assyria sent Rabshakeh from Lachish to Jerusalem unto king Hezekiah with a great army. And he stood by the conduit of the upper pool in the highway of the fuller's field.

"Then came forth unto him Eliakim, Hilkiah's son, which was over the house, and Shebna the scribe, and Joah, Asaph's son, the recorder.

"And Rabshakeh said unto them, Say ye now to Hezekiah, Thus saith the great king, the king of Assyria, What confidence is this wherein thou trustest? I say, sayest thou, (but they are but vain words) I have counsel and strength for war: now on whom dost thou trust, that thou rebellest against me?

"Lo, thou trustest in the staff of this broken reed, on Egypt; whereon if a man lean, it will go into his hand, and pierce it: so is Pharaoh king of Egypt to all that trust in him. But if thou say to me, We trust in the Lord our God: is it not he, whose high places and whose altars Hezekiah hath taken away, and said to Judah and to Jerusalem, Ye shall worship before this altar?

"Now therefore give pledges, I pray thee, to my master the king of Assyria, and I will give thee two thousand horses, if thou be able on thy part to set riders upon them.

"How then wilt thou turn away the face of one captain of the least of my master's servants, and put thy trust on Egypt for chariots and for horsemen? And am I now come up without the Lord against this land to destroy it? the Lord said unto me, Go up against this land, and destroy it.

"Then said Eliakim and Shebna and Joah unto Rabshakeh, Speak, I pray thee, unto thy servants in the Syrian language; for we understand it; and speak not to us in the Jews' language, in the ears of the people that are on the wall.

"But Rabshakeh said, Hath my master sent me to thy master and to thee to speak these words? hath he not sent me to the men that sit upon the wall, that they may eat their own dung, and drink their own piss with you?

"Then Rabshakeh stood, and cried with a loud voice in the Jews' language, and said, Hear ye the words of the great king, the king of Assyria.

"Thus saith the king, Let not Hezekiah deceive you: for he shall not be able to deliver you. Neither let Hezekiah make you trust in the Lord, saying, The Lord will surely deliver us: this city shall not be delivered into the hand of the king of Assyria.

"Hearken not to Hezekiah: for thus saith the king of Assyria, Make an agreement with me by a present, and come out to me: and eat ye every one of his vine, and every one of his fig tree, and drink ye every one the waters of his own cistern; until I come and take you away to a land like your own land, a land of corn and wine, a land of bread and vineyards.

"Beware lest Hezekiah persuade you, saying, The Lord will deliver us. Hath any of the gods of the nations delivered his land out of the hand of the king of Assyria? Where are the gods of Hamath and Arphad? where are the gods of Sepharvaim? and have they delivered Samaria out of my hand? Who are they among all the gods of these lands, that have delivered their land out of my hand, that the Lord should deliver Jerusalem out of my hand?

"But they held their peace, and answered him not a word: for the king's commandment was, saying, Answer him not." (Isaiah 36:1-21.)

Isaiah's response to the situation is contained in the following:

"Therefore thus saith the Lord concerning the king of Assyria, He shall not come into this city, nor shoot an arrow there, nor come before it with shields, nor cast a bank against it.

"By the way that he came, by the same shall he return, and shall not come into this city, saith the Lord. For I will defend this city to save it for mine own sake, and for my servant David's sake.

"Then the angel of the Lord went forth, and smote in the camp of the Assyrians a hundred and fourscore and five thousand: and when they arose early in the morning, behold, they were all dead corpses.

"So Sennacherib king of Assyria departed, and went and returned, and dwelt at Nineveh. And it came to pass, as he was worshipping in the house of Nisroch his god, that Adrammelech and Sharezer his sons smote him with the sword; and they escaped into the land of Armenia: and Esarhaddon his son reigned in his stead." (Isaiah 37:33-38.)

Chapter Seven

HEZEKIAH'S ILLNESS

A severe illness came to Hezekiah, and he was "sick unto death." Then it was that Isaiah came to him and said, "Set thine house in order: for thou shalt die, and not live." (Isaiah 38:1.)

But Hezekiah did not want to die. He turned his face toward the wall as he lay in bed and prayed, saying:

"Remember now, O Lord, I beseech thee, how I have walked before thee in truth and with a perfect heart, and have done that which is good in thy sight. And Hezekiah wept sore.

"Then came the word of the Lord to Isaiah, saying, Go, and say to Hezekiah, Thus saith the Lord, the God of David thy father, I have heard thy prayer, I have seen thy tears: behold, I will add unto thy days fifteen years. And I will deliver thee and this city out of the hand of the king of Assyria: and I will defend this city. And this shall be a sign unto thee from the Lord, that the Lord will do this thing that he hath spoken." (Isaiah 38:3-7.)

At this time Isaiah predicted the Babylonian captivity. Following Hezekiah's recovery, the king of Babylon sent letters and messengers with gifts to him, "for he had heard that he had been sick, and was recovered. And Hezekiah was glad of them, and shewed them the house of his precious things, the silver, and the gold, and the spices, and the precious ointment, and all the house of his armour, and all that was found in his treasures: there was nothing in his house, nor in all his dominion, that Hezekiah shewed them not.

"Then came Isaiah the prophet unto king Hezekiah, and said unto him, What said these men? and from whence came they unto thee? And Hezekiah said, They are come from a far country unto me, even from Babylon.

"Then said he, What have they seen in thine house? And Hezekiah answered, All that is in mine house have they seen: there is nothing among my treasures that I have not shewed them.

"Then said Isaiah to Hezekiah, Hear the word of the Lord of hosts; Behold, the days come, that all that is in thine house, and that which thy fathers have laid up in store until this day, shall be carried to Babylon: nothing shall be left, saith the Lord. And of thy sons that shall issue from thee, which thou shalt beget, shall they take away; and they shall be eunuchs in the palace of the king of Babylon." (Isaiah 39:1-7.)

Isaiah also predicted the eventual doom of Babylon. He said:

"Behold, I will stir up the Medes against them, which shall not regard silver; and as for gold, they shall not delight in it. Their bows also shall dash the young men to pieces; and they shall have no pity on the fruit of the womb; their eye shall not spare children.

"And Babylon, the glory of kingdoms, the beauty of the Chaldees' excellency, shall be as when God overthrew Sodom and Gomorrah. It shall never be inhabited, neither shall it be dwelt in from generation to generation: neither shall the Arabian pitch tent there; neither shall the shepherds make their fold there.

"But wild beasts of the desert shall lie there; and their houses shall be full of doleful creatures; and owls shall dwell there, and satyrs shall dance there. And the wild beasts of the islands shall cry in their desolate houses, and dragons in their pleasant palaces: and her time is near to come, and her days shall not be prolonged." (Isaiah 13:17-22.)

This literally happened. Babylon was never rebuilt; today it is but a desolation.

Hezekiah lived for the additional fifteen years. On

his death he was given the highest of honors by his people. The Talmudists write that he had been such a righteous man that many thought he was the long-looked-for Messiah. They also say that the reason he pleaded so earnestly to live longer was that he had no male heir to inherit the throne.

However, after his recovery, according to the Jewish writers, the king married one of the daughters of the prophet Isaiah who bore to him a male child, Manasseh. It was this Manasseh who restored idolatry and who later killed Isaiah by "sawing him asunder."

Manasseh was only twelve years old when he ascended the throne, but as he grew older he brought back all the idolatrous practices of his predecessor Ahaz, and Judah again apostatized from the Lord.

Isaiah continued his ministry, constantly warning Manasseh against his grievous sins. This led to enmity between the prophet and the king who ultimately ordered his execution.

Chapter Eight

ISAIAH SAW GOD!

The prophet Isaiah saw God! His testimony of the Almighty is vivid, great, and firm.

He not only saw the Lord, but he also heard his voice—frequently and repeatedly. Indeed, Isaiah was a prophet, a seer, and a revelator in the truest sense. He testifies:

"In the year that king Uzziah died I saw also the Lord sitting upon a throne, high and lifted up, and his train filled the temple. Above it stood the seraphims: each one had six wings; with twain he covered his face, and with twain he covered his feet, and with twain he did fly. And one cried unto another, and said, Holy, holy, holy, is the Lord of hosts: the whole earth is full of his glory. And the posts of the door moved at the voice of him that cried, and the house was filled with smoke." (Isaiah 6:1-4.)

It is of more than ordinary interest that the first Nephi in the Book of Mormon testified also that Isaiah saw God. Said he:

"And now I, Nephi, write more of the words of Isaiah, for my soul delighteth in his words. For I will liken his words unto my people, and I will send them forth unto all my children, for he verily saw my Redeemer, even as I have seen him.

"And my brother, Jacob, also has seen him as I have seen him; wherefore, I will send their words forth unto my children to prove unto them that my words are true. Wherefore, by the words of three, God hath said, I will establish my word. Nevertheless, God sendeth more witnesses, and he proveth all his words." (2 Nephi 11:2-3.)

There was good reason why Nephi thus quoted Isaiah; he continued:

"Behold, my soul delighteth in proving unto my people the truth of the coming of Christ; for, for this end hath the law of Moses been given; and all things which have been given of God from the beginning of the world, unto man, are the typifying of him.

"And also my soul delighteth in the covenants of the Lord which he hath made to our fathers; yea, my soul delighteth in his grace, and in his justice, and power, and mercy in the great and eternal plan of deliverance from death.

"And my soul delighteth in proving unto my people that save Christ should come all men must perish." (2 Nephi 11:4-6.)

Nephi thus gives convincing validity to the testimony of Isaiah. Nephi's reason for quoting the Jewish prophet was simply and directly to prove that Christ would come. Both Nephi and his brother Jacob had seen the Christ. They testified that Isaiah also saw the Lord, and thus did these three witnesses join together to prove the reality of the Savior.

Note again that Nephi used Isaiah as proof of what he himself said. Nephi used him to convince the Nephites that Jesus Christ is the Savior, for Isaiah had also seen Him. Nephi's use of that prophet's testimony proves also some of the essential facts about Isaiah:

He was a prophet of God.

His writings were known to Nephi.

He did see God, and Nephi had that fact made known to him by the scriptures.

He did bear a strong written testimony, which Nephi fully accepted.

Isaiah's description of his view of the Deity is similar to that given by the prophet Amos concerning his vision. Said that prophet: "I saw the Lord standing upon the altar." Then he described what the Lord said to him. (Amos 9:1.)

Isaiah saw the Lord sitting upon his throne, and Amos saw him standing above the altar.

When the Savior appeared to Joseph Smith and Oliver Cowdery in the Kirtland Temple, he stood "upon the breastwork of the pulpit, before us; and under his feet was a paved work of pure gold, in color like amber." (D&C 110:2.)

Moses and the seventy elders saw him similarly. The record says: "Then went up Moses, and Aaron, Nadab, and Abihu, and seventy of the elders of Israel: And they saw the God of Israel: and there was under his feet as it were a paved work of a sapphire stone, and as it were the body of heaven in his clearness. And upon the nobles of the children of Israel he laid not his hand: also they saw God, and did eat and drink." (Exodus 24:9-11.)

Of this Moses wrote further, saying: "And ye said, Behold, the Lord our God hath shewed us his glory and his greatness, and we have heard his voice out of the midst of the fire: we have seen this day that God doth talk with man, and he liveth." (Deuteronomy 5:24.)

Paul spoke of the Savior, also upon a throne beside his Father. He wrote to the Hebrews: "God, who at sundry times and in diverse manners spake in time past unto the fathers by the prophets, hath in these last days spoken unto us by his Son, whom he hath appointed heir of all things, by whom also he made the worlds; who being the brightness of his glory, and the express image of his person, and upholding all things by the word of his power, when he had by himself purged our sins, sat down on the right hand of the Majesty on high." (Hebrews 1:1-3.)

Those who question that Isaiah saw God should learn that all the Bible versions confirm it, from the Masoretic text to the Roman Catholic Jerusalem Bible.

It is confirmed in the Inspired Version by Joseph Smith; it is declared in the Holy Scriptures by the Jehovah's Witnesses.

The Masoretic text says, "In the year that King Uzziah died I saw the Lord sitting upon a throne high and lifted up, and His train filled the temple.''

The New World Translation of Jehovah's Witnesses says, ''In the year that King Uzziah died I, however, got to see Jehovah, sitting on a throne lofty and lifted up.''

The Jerusalem Bible says, ''In the year of King Uzziah's death I saw the Lord Yahweh seated on a high throne; his train filled the sanctuary.''

Each of the versions says that Isaiah not only saw the Lord, but that the Lord also spoke to him and gave him revelation. ''Also I heard the voice of the Lord,'' he says. (Isaiah 6:8.)

Repeatedly throughout his book, Isaiah speaks of hearing the voice of the Lord and of receiving instruction from him that he passed on to the people.

The book of Isaiah opens with an immediate reference to one of the prophet's great visions. Isaiah writes: ''Hear, O heavens, and give ear, O earth: for the Lord hath spoken.'' (Isaiah 1:2.)

At another time the prophet said: ''Moreover the Lord said unto me, Take thee a great roll, and write in it with a man's pen. . . .'' (Isaiah 8:1.)

In the same chapter he writes, ''For the Lord spake thus to me with a strong hand, and instructed me that I should not walk in the way of this people.'' (Verse 11.)

Isaiah spoke as one having authority, directly as the mouthpiece of God, as for example: ''Wherefore thus saith the Holy One of Israel,'' and ''thus saith the Lord God, the Holy One of Israel.'' (Isaiah 30:12, 15.)

As Isaiah spoke the word of the Lord, he did so with courage and conviction. There was no hesitation in his mind. He spoke plainly, exposing the sins of the people and calling them to repentance. He predicted the scattering as well as the gathering of Israel, and bore his continuous testimony to the Holy One of Israel, whom he identified as both Savior and Redeemer.

Chapter Nine

HE TESTIFIED OF CHRIST

Without doubt, one of the most moving portions of all the writings of Isaiah is chapter 53, wherein he describes the labors and sufferings of the Savior.

Isaiah understood the atonement of Christ. It was no mystery to him. And he wrote of it with the deepest of feeling. "Who hath believed our report," he begins, "and to whom is the arm of the Lord revealed?" (Verse 1.)

Indeed, it may seem difficult to believe Isaiah's prediction—or his report—that the Savior would suffer so for mankind, or even that he, the Creator, would be without comeliness. "When we shall see him, there is no beauty that we should desire him." (Verse 2.)

Jesus was both Jehovah and Creator. Could such a mighty Personage be without comeliness? Apparently he was during his mortality. It was when the Savior was transfigured that "the fashion of his countenance was altered, and his raiment was white and glistening." Thus he became glorious in his appearance. But only Peter, James, and John were allowed to see him so. (Luke 9:29.)

In his mortal life he looked so much like other men that his crucifiers could not identify him from among the disciples, and so they hired Judas for thirty pieces of silver to point him out to them.

How true were Isaiah's words: "He is despised and rejected of men; a man of sorrows, and acquainted with grief: and we hid as it were our faces from him; he was despised, and we esteemed him not." (Isaiah 53:3.)

How he was jeered, ridiculed, and spat upon!

How many times was he accused of being a devil, or of being possessed of a devil! His critics called him names, even Beelzebub, whom the Jews believed to be the prince of evil spirits. The Pharisees cried out: "This fellow doth not cast out devils, but by Beelzebub the prince of the devils." What was Jesus' response? "If Satan cast out Satan, he is divided against himself; how shall then his kingdom stand?" (Matthew 12:24, 26.)

The Lord comforted his persecuted disciples by saying, "If they have called the master of the house Beelzebub, how much more shall they call them of his household?" (Matthew 10:25.)

Isaiah spoke of the atonement itself: "Surely he hath borne our griefs, and carried our sorrows: yet we did esteem him stricken, smitten of God, and afflicted." (Isaiah 53:4.)

Some of his closest disciples doubted him at first, but more so when he was arrested and later crucified. They fled when he was seized by the mob led by Judas. And on the third day, which should have been important to them, they would not believe the women who reported his resurrection. Even as they themselves looked at him after his resurrection, some still doubted until he said: "Handle me, and see; for a spirit hath not flesh and bones, as ye see me have." (Luke 24:39.)

"But he was wounded for our transgressions, he was bruised for our iniquities; the chastisement of our peace was upon him; and with his stripes we are healed." (Isaiah 53:5.)

Was a more descriptive statement of the atonement ever given? Christ was the Savior! He died for us! He paid the price of our transgressions, "and with his stripes we are healed."

But there are those who give it little heed. "All we like sheep have gone astray; we have turned every one to his own way." How true this is of so many. And yet he is the Redeemer, "and the Lord hath laid on him the iniquity of us all." (Verse 6.)

Can we ever forget the scriptural account of his suffering in Gethsemane, or his sweating drops of blood? Can we ignore his agony on the cross? Can we set aside his own words as he told of his suffering?

"For behold, I, God, have suffered these things for all, that they might not suffer if they would repent; But if they would not repent they must suffer even as I; which suffering caused myself, even God, the greatest of all, to tremble because of pain, and to bleed at every pore, and to suffer both body and spirit—and would that I might not drink the bitter cup, and shrink." (D&C 19:16-18.)

It was the iniquity of us all that caused him this suffering. Yet, as Savior and Redeemer, he humbly said, "The cup which my Father hath given me, shall I not drink it?" (John 18:11.)

In modern revelation he added: "Nevertheless, glory be to the Father, and I partook and finished my preparations unto the children of men." (D&C 19:19.)

Evidently foreseeing the attitude of Jesus before the high priests who demanded his crucifixion, and those who condemned him, Isaiah said: "He was oppressed, and he was afflicted, yet he opened not his mouth: he is brought as a lamb to the slaughter, and as a sheep before her shearers is dumb, so he openeth not his mouth." (Isaiah 53:7.)

The Savior said little to Pilate, and less to the high priests. But he did declare his divine Sonship!

"He was taken from prison and from judgment: and who shall declare his generation? for he was cut off out of the land of the living: for the transgression of my people was he stricken." (Verse 8.)

It is of more than ordinary moment that Isaiah wrote this: "And he made his grave with the wicked, and with the rich in his death; because he had done no violence, neither was any deceit in his mouth." (Verse 9.)

He died with thieves; he was buried in a rich man's tomb, and the soldiers divided his raiment between them.

"Yet it pleased the Lord to bruise him; he hath put

him to grief: when thou shalt make his soul an offering for sin, he shall see his seed, he shall prolong his days, and the pleasure of the Lord shall prosper in his hand.

"He shall see of the travail of his soul, and shall be satisfied: by his knowledge shall my righteous servant justify many; for he shall bear their iniquities.

"Therefore will I divide him a portion with the great, and he shall divide the spoil with the strong; because he hath poured out his soul unto death: and he was numbered with the transgressors; and he bare the sin of many, and made intercession for the transgressors." (Verses 10-12.)

What a description of the Savior in his atonement! What a revelation! What a testimony!

Chapter Ten

PREDICTIONS OF CHRIST

No biblical prophet foretold the coming of the Savior more clearly than did Isaiah. In great detail he described his mission. He saw that the Lord would be born of a virgin, and he detailed the manner of His death and burial. "Behold, a virgin shall conceive, and bear a son, and shall call his name Immanuel." (Isaiah 7:14.)

Matthew records the fulfillment in these words:

"Now the birth of Jesus Christ was on this wise: When as his mother Mary was espoused to Joseph, before they came together, she was found with child of the Holy Ghost.

"Then Joseph her husband, being a just man, and not willing to make her a publick example, was minded to put her away privily.

"But while he thought on these things, behold, the angel of the Lord appeared unto him in a dream, saying, Joseph, thou son of David, fear not to take unto thee Mary thy wife: for that which is conceived in her is of the Holy Ghost.

"And she shall bring forth a son, and thou shalt call his name JESUS: for he shall save his people from their sins.

"Now all this was done, that it might be fulfilled which was spoken of the Lord by the prophet, saying,

"Behold, a virgin shall be with child, and shall bring forth a son, and they shall call his name Emmanuel, which being interpreted is, God with us." (Matthew 1:18-23.)

Isn't it significant that "his name shall be called Immanuel"? Who was the Babe of Bethlehem? He was the

Creator of all the heavens and the earth. He was Jehovah of the Old Testament and Christ of the New Testament. He was the Son of Almighty God!

Did he change his identity when he was born into mortality? No! None of us do. We all retain our identity from the premortal existence through this mortal life and on into immorality hereafter. Could it be otherwise?

Neither did Jesus change into a different being. He was the divine Jehovah before his birth. He was the divine Jehovah after his mortal birth. He was the Beloved Son of God before coming into mortality. He was so in mortality. Did not the Father identify him thus, both at his baptism and on the Mount of Transfiguration?

"This is my beloved Son, in whom I am well pleased" was the declaration as Jesus came up from the waters of baptism. (Matthew 3:17.) And, "This is my beloved Son, in whom I am well pleased; hear ye him" was the acknowledgment of the Father on the mount. (Matthew 17:5.)

It was the self-same Well-Beloved Son who had brought about the creations of the heavens. The Almighty said to Moses, even when Moses was still in mortality, and long before the birth of Christ: "And behold, the glory of the Lord was upon Moses, so that Moses stood in the presence of God, and talked with him face to face. And the Lord God said unto Moses: For mine own purpose have I made these things. Here is wisdom and it remaineth in me.

"And by the word of my power, have I created them, which is mine Only Begotten Son, who is full of grace and truth.

"And worlds without number have I created; and I also created them for mine own purpose; and by the Son I created them, which is mine Only Begotten." (Moses 1:31-33.)

Jesus in truth was the Only Begotten of the Father in the flesh, and the Father himself indentified him as such both before and after his birth—while he was yet in the premortal life, and also while he was in mortality. And he did so after the resurrection in addressing the Nephites. (3 Nephi 11:7.) He is yet to come as the returning Christ in his glorious second coming, and he will still be the very same mighty Personage.

Wasn't he the same Being who appeared to the Nephites after his resurrection in Palestine? Did he not say to them, "Behold I am Jesus Christ," and did he not allow them to examine the marks of the crucifixion? (3 Nephi 11:6-17.)

Jesus never changed his identity. He came into this world as the child of Mary and the Son of God. He was divine before coming into mortality, and in mortality he was called "Emmanuel, which being interpreted is, God with us." (Matthew 1:23.)

The ancient prophet wrote of the mercy and kindness of the Lord: "He shall feed his flock like a shepherd: he shall gather the lambs with his arm, and carry them in his bosom, and shall gently lead those that are with young." (Isaiah 40:11.)

Isaiah described the mighty works of the Savior before he ever came to earth, and asked:

"Who hath measured the waters in the hollow of his hand, and meted out heaven with the span, and comprehended the dust of the earth in a measure, and weighed the mountains in scales, and the hills in a balance?

"Who hath directed the Spirit of the Lord, or being his counseller hath taught him?

"With whom took he counsel, and who instructed him, and taught him in the path of judgment, and taught him knowledge, and shewed to him the way of understanding?

"Behold, the nations are as a drop of a bucket, and are counted as the small dust of the balance: behold, he taketh up the isles as a very little thing." (Isaiah 40:12-15.)

When Isaiah wrote what is the eleventh chapter of his book, he referred to "a rod out of the stem of Jesse, and a Branch shall grow out of his roots." (Verse 1.)

By revelation the Prophet Joseph Smith identified this passage as a further declaration of the forthcoming mortal birth of the Christ. He inquired of the Lord for the meaning of that scripture and the Lord replied:

"Who is the Stem of Jesse spoken of in the 1st, 2d, 3d, 4th, and 5th verses of the 11th chapter of Isaiah?

"Verily thus saith the Lord: It is Christ.

"What is the rod spoken of in the first verse of the 11th chapter of Isaiah, that should come of the Stem of Jesse?

"Behold, thus saith the Lord: It is a servant in the hands of Christ, who is partly a descendant of Jesse as well as of Ephraim, or of the house of Joseph, on whom there is laid much power.

"What is the root of Jesse spoken of in the 10th verse of the 11th chapter?

"Behold, thus saith the Lord, it is a descendant of Jesse, as well as of Joseph, unto whom rightly belongs the priesthood, and the keys of the kingdom, for an ensign, and for the gathering of my people in the last days.

"Questions by Elias Higbee: What is meant by the command in Isaiah, 52d chapter, 1st verse, which saith: Put on thy strength, O Zion—and what people had Isaiah reference to?

"He had reference to those whom God should call in the last days, who should hold the power of priesthood to bring again Zion, and the redemption of Israel; and to put on her strength is to put on the authority of the priesthood, which she, Zion, has a right to by lineage; also to return to that power which she had lost.

"What are we to understand by Zion loosing herself from the bands of her neck; 2d verse?

"We are to understand that the scattered remnants are exhorted to return to the Lord from whence they have fallen; which if they do, the promise of the Lord is that he will speak to them, or give them revelation. See the 6th, 7th, and 8th verses. The bands of her neck are the curses of God upon her, or the remnants of Israel in their scattered condition among the Gentiles." (D&C 113.)

Isaiah describes him further and says:

"And the spirit of the Lord shall rest upon him, the spirit of wisdom and understanding, the spirit of counsel and might, the spirit of knowledge and of the fear of the Lord;

"And shall make him of quick understanding in the fear of the Lord: and he shall not judge after the sight of his eyes, neither reprove after the hearing of his ears:

"But with righteousness shall he judge the poor, and reprove with equity for the meek of the earth: and he shall smite the earth with the rod of his mouth, and with the breath of his lips shall he slay the wicked.

"And righteousness shall be the girdle of his loins, and faithfulness the girdle of his reins.

"The wolf also shall dwell with the lamb, and the leopard shall lie down with the kid; and the calf and the young lion and the fatling together; and a little child shall lead them.

"And the cow and the bear shall feed; their young ones shall lie down together: and the lion shall eat straw like the ox.

"And the sucking child shall play on the hole of the asp, and the weaned child shall put his hand on the cockatrice' den.

"They shall not hurt nor destroy in all my holy mountain: for the earth shall be full of the knowledge of the Lord, as the waters cover the sea." (Isaiah 11:2-9.)

Speaking of the latter days when these peaceful conditions will prevail, Isaiah tells of the gathering of Israel:

"And in that day there shall be a root of Jesse, which shall stand for an ensign of the people; to it shall the Gentiles seek: and his rest shall be glorious.

"And it shall come to pass in that day, that the Lord shall set his hand again the second time to recover the remnant of his people, which shall be left, from Assyria, and from Egypt, and from Pathros, and from Cush, and from Elam, and from Shinar, and from Hamath, and from the islands of the sea.

"And he shall set up an ensign for the nations, and shall assemble the outcasts of Israel, and gather together the dispersed of Judah from the four corners of the earth. . . .

"And there shall be an highway for the remnant of his people, which shall be left, from Assyria; like as it was to Israel in the day that he came up out of the land of Egypt." (Isaiah 11:10-12, 16.)

Further speaking of the Christ, Isaiah then provides us with one of his great poetic compositions:

And in that day thou shalt say,
O Lord, I will praise thee:
Though thou wast angry with me,
Thine anger is turned away,
And thou comfortedst me.

Behold, God is my salvation;
I will trust, and not be afraid:
For the Lord Jehovah is my strength
And my song; he also is become my
Salvation.
Therefore with joy shall ye draw
Water out of the wells of salvation.

And in that day shall ye say,
Praise the Lord, call upon his name,
Declare his doings among the people,
Make mention that his name is exalted.

Sing unto the Lord;
For he hath done excellent things:
This is known in all the earth.

Cry out and shout,
Thou inhabitants of Zion:
For great is the Holy One of Israel
In the midst of thee. (Isaiah 12.)

This poem reminds us of the psalms of David, it is so expressive, so beautifully written, so devout and worshipful. Many of Isaiah's chapters are regarded as true poetry, just as are the psalms.

Some of the newer versions of the Bible, and especially the rendering in the Masoretic text, set his words as poetry in chapter after chapter. In chapter 12 he certainly is at his best.

Chapter Eleven

ISAIAH AND ABINADI

One of the most courageous of the prophets was Abinadi of the Book of Mormon. He was a faithful student of Isaiah and quoted him generously.

As Abinadi faced death before King Noah, he resorted to Isaiah for his greatest declaration: that the Christ will come. He quoted the 53rd chapter of Isaiah to the wicked king and his priests and challenged them to accept the Christ and turn from their evil ways. "Yea," he began, "even doth not Isaiah say. . . ." (Mosiah 14:1.) And then he quoted Isaiah 53 essentially as it appears in the King James Translation of the Bible.

Was not Abinadi testifying of Christ? Did he not use Isaiah as a witness for Christ? Every word testifies of Jesus. Did not Isaiah speak the truth? Was he not inspired, even as was Abinadi? Would Abinadi have quoted him if Isaiah was not inspired?

But Abinadi went further in testifying of Christ and in giving full validity to the testimony of Isaiah. This Book of Mormon prophet declared that God did give the "Son power to make intercession for the children of men" (Mosiah 15:8), and he declared that the resurrection would be brought about by this Savior of whom Isaiah testified.

Abinadi announced the very name of Christ, saying, "for so shall he be called." (Mosiah 15:21.) Speaking of the resurrection he said:

"They are raised to dwell with God who has redeemed them; thus they have eternal life through Christ, who has broken the bands of death.

"And these are those who have part in the first resurrection; and these are they that have died before Christ came, in their ignorance, not having salvation unto them. And thus the Lord bringeth about the restoration of these; and they have a part in the first resurrection, or have eternal life, being redeemed by the Lord.

"And little children also have eternal life." (Mosiah 15:23-25.)

So Isaiah was instrumental in sustaining the doctrine of Christ even in ancient America through this and other Book of Morman quotations.

Isaiah firmly declared the Christ as the Savior of the world. Among other things he said: "Thus saith the Lord . . . I, even I, am the Lord; and beside me there is no saviour." (Isaiah 43:1, 11.)

It will be recalled that Peter used similar language as he addressed the high priests in Jerusalem:

"Be it known unto you all, and to all the people of Israel, that by the name of Jesus Christ of Nazareth, whom ye crucified, whom God raised from the dead, even by him doth this man stand here before you whole.

"This is the stone which was set at nought of you builders, which is become the head of the corner.

"Neither is there salvation in any other: for there is none other name under heaven given among men, whereby we must be saved." (Acts 4:10-12.)

Peter went further in his own defense as he faced the wicked rulers of Jerusalem who had demanded that he no longer speak the name of Christ.

"Then Peter and the other apostles answered and said, We ought to obey God rather than men. The God of our fathers raised up Jesus, whom ye slew and hanged on a tree. Him hath God exalted with his right hand to be a Prince and a Saviour, for to give repentance to Israel, and forgiveness of sins. And we are his witnesses of these things; and so is also the Holy Ghost, whom God hath given to them that obey him." (Acts 5:29-32.)

Again the words of the Lord to Isaiah identified the Christ: "Tell ye, and bring them near; yea, let them take counsel together: who hath declared this from ancient time? who hath told it from that time? have not I the Lord? and there is no God else beside me; a just God and a Saviour; there is none beside me." (Isaiah 45:21.)

Speaking of the divine Redeemer, who alone is Jesus Christ, Isaiah said this: "For thy Maker is thine husband; the Lord of hosts is his name; and thy Redeemer the Holy One of Israel; The God of the whole earth shall he be called. . . . In a little wrath I hid my face from thee for a moment; but with everlasting kindness will I have mercy on thee, saith the Lord thy Redeemer." (Isaiah 54:5, 8.) Note his frequent use of the titles "Redeemer" and "Savior," which are applicable only to Jesus of Nazareth.

Can anyone mistake such scriptures? Did not Isaiah abundantly testify of Christ?

Is it any wonder that the Savior commanded us to read Isaiah, "For great are the words of Isaiah"?

When it is realized that salvation comes alone through Jesus, and Isaiah was so vocal in declaring this fact, it becomes essential that all people understand and believe him.

As Isaiah spoke of the Lord and his atonement, he taught clearly that mankind, through Him, may receive forgiveness of sins. He appealed to the people of his day in such terms and said:

"Come now, and let us reason together, saith the Lord: though your sins be as scarlet, they shall be as white as snow; though they be red like crimson, they shall be as wool.

"If ye be willing and obedient, ye shall eat the good of the land: But if ye refuse and rebel, ye shall be devoured with the sword: for the mouth of the Lord hath spoken it." (Isaiah 1:18-20.)

He said further: "Fear not, thou worm Jacob, and ye men of Israel; I will help thee, saith the Lord, and thy redeemer, the Holy One of Israel." (Isaiah 41:14.)

He revealed that the atonement paid the price of sin:

"I, even I, am he that blotteth out thy transgressions for mine own sake, and will not remember thy sins." (Isaiah 43:25.)

He spoke of the resurrection, which alone comes through Jesus, and said: "Thy dead men shall live, together with my dead body shall they arise. Awake and sing, ye that dwell in dust: for thy dew is as the dew of herbs, and the earth shall cast out the dead." (Isaiah 26:19.)

He spoke repeatedly of the second coming of the Lord, of which the following is an example: "Behold, the Lord God will come with strong hand, and his arm shall rule for him: behold, his reward is with him, and his work before him." (Isaiah 40:10.)

And he added: "For, behold, the Lord will come with fire, and with his chariots like a whirlwind, to render his anger with fury, and his rebuke with flames of fire. For by fire and by his sword will the Lord plead with all flesh: and the slain of the Lord shall be many." (Isaiah 66:15-16.)

But always he assured the righteous of peace, protection, and rich rewards.

Chapter Twelve

"WONDERFUL, COUNSELLER"

One of the most pointed predictions of the coming of Christ appearing anywhere in the Old Testament is Isaiah's declaration, which reads: "For unto us a child is born, unto us a son is given: and the government shall be upon his shoulder: and his name shall be called Wonderful, Counseller, The mighty God, The everlasting Father, The Prince of Peace." (Isaiah 9:6.)

This immediately establishes the divine nature of the Savior. He is the Mighty God.

To affirm the divinity of Jesus is basic to our faith. It is the faithless who question that he is Deity. It is the faithless who raise doubts, just as they did in the day when he lived.

"Is not this the carpenter's son?" they asked. "Is not his Mother called Mary? And his brethren, James, and Joses, and Simon, and Judas? And his sisters, are they not all with us? When then hath this man all these things?" (Matthew 13:55-56.)

Even within the immediate family of Jesus there was unbelief. Mary knew his identity, for the angel had declared it unto her. And Joseph, her husband, had been similarly informed. But Mary evidently did not broadcast her knowledge; she "kept all these things, and pondered them in her heart." (Luke 2:19.)

Her other sons, born to her by Joseph, did not believe, at least not at first. They had grown up with Jesus. He was their older brother. They had become so accustomed to him as they all grew up together that they saw nothing unusual about him, certainly nothing divine. Jesus was so much like other men that not even his own blood brothers recognized his true status.

This was revealed in the scripture telling of their visit to Jerusalem for the Passover. The brothers planned to attend and wondered if Jesus would go also. It is not indicated whether they invited him to accompany them to Jerusalem. They knew of his reported miracles, but seemed to doubt them. They knew he had been persecuted and hence had shunned the crowds in Jerusalem.

They said to him, "Depart hence, and go into Judea that thy disciples also may see the works that thou doest. For there is no man that doeth any thing in secret, and he himself seeketh to be known openly."

Then they daringly added, "If thou do these things, shew thyself to the world." Note that "if." How much did they really doubt him? It seems that they even taunted him, "For neither did his brethren believe in him."

Jesus did not hesitate to reply, saying, "My time is not yet come: but your time is alway ready. The world cannot hate you." (John 7:4-7.)

Was that because they did not believe in him, and thus they were "of" the world and the world "would love his own"? (John 15:19.)

"The world cannot hate you; but me it hateth, because I testify of it, that the works thereof are evil." (John 7:7.)

And yet Isaiah said that he was the Mighty God, and called him Immanuel, "God with us." When was he the Mighty God? He never departed from that status!

He was the mighty God in the creation, as the babe in Bethlehem, at his baptism, and as he walked the plains of Palestine.

He was the Savior when he talked to the woman of Samaria who referred to the coming Messiah. It was then that he said, "I that speak unto thee am he." (John 4:26.)

He was the Redeemer when he administered the sacrament of the Lord's Supper to his disciples and told them to partake subsequently in remembrance of him.

He was the Creator and the Savior as he debated with

the lawyers and scribes, as he was also when he was betrayed by Judas.

He was the divine Son of God as he stood before the high priests and the Roman governor. And so he was during his trial when the high priest asked him, "Art thou the Christ, the Son of the Blessed?" And the Lord replied, "I am." (Mark 14:61-62.)

He was divine while on the cross, atoning for the sins of all mankind. His sacrifice was beyond human comprehension, not to mention any human ability to endure.

He was divine as he came forth from the tomb, breaking the bands of death, bringing to pass the resurrection, not only for himself but for all mankind. Truly, "as in Adam all die, even so in Christ shall all be made alive." (1 Corinthians 15:22.)

He was still the great Immanuel as he showed himself to his disciples after the resurrection, and later as he allowed twenty-five hundred Nephites to feel the marks of the crucifixion, and as he ascended to heaven.

And he is God today. He it was who came with our Eternal Father to the youthful Joseph Smith. He it was who was introduced by the Father to Joseph, saying, "This is My Beloved Son. Hear Him!" (Joseph Smith–History 1:17.)

He it is who has established his church in these last days, and whose servants carry his word to every nation, kindred, tongue, and people, as the prophets foretold.

Yes, Jesus of Nazareth truly is the Mighty God, the Savior and Redeemer, Immanuel, Wonderful, the Prince of Peace, the Only Begotten Son of our Father in heaven.

Chapter Thirteen

HOPE FOR THE DEAD

As Isaiah testified of Christ, he opened to his readers still another view of the divine Son of God. He declared that Jesus would pierce the doors of the prison house and provide salvation for the dead as well as for the living. He was the first of the biblical prophets to speak of this subject.

It will be remembered that Jesus, during his travels, came to Nazareth, his childhood city. As was his custom, he went to the synagogue on the Sabbath and read to the congregation from the scripture.

"And there was delivered unto him the book of the prophet Esaias. And when he had opened the book, he found the place where it was written,

"The Spirit of the Lord is upon me, because he hath anointed me to preach the gospel to the poor; he hath sent me to heal the brokenhearted, to preach deliverance to the captives, and recovering of sight to the blind, to set at liberty them that are bruised, to preach the acceptable year of the Lord.

"And he closed the book, and he gave it again to the minister, and sat down. And the eyes of all them that were in the synagogue were fastened on him. And he began to say unto them, This day is this scripture fulfilled in your ears." (Luke 4:17-21.)

But as he preached to them, "all they in the synagogue, when they heard these things, were filled with wrath, and rose up, and thrust him out of the city, and led him unto the brow of the hill whereon their city was built, that they might cast him down headlong. But he passing through the midst of them went his way." (Luke 4:28-30.)

He quoted from Isaiah. When he said "This day is this scripture fulfilled in your ears," he identified himself as that Being referred to by Isaiah.

But the people in the synagogue would not accept him, and again asked, "Is not this Joseph's son?" In response to their rejection he said, "No prophet is accepted in his own country." (Luke 4:22-24.)

Jesus would not only teach the living, bind up the brokenhearted, and preach good tidings to the meek; he would also "proclaim liberty to the captives, and the opening of the prison to them that are bound." (Isaiah 61:1.)

Isaiah had said something similar in an early chapter:

"I the Lord have called thee in righteousness, and will hold thine hand, and will keep thee, and give thee for a covenant of the people, for a light of the Gentiles; to open the blind eyes, to bring out the prisoners from the prison, and them that sit in darkness out of the prison house.

"I am the Lord: that is my name: and my glory will I not give to another, neither my praise to graven images." (Isaiah 42:6-8.)

And how did the Savior bring deliverance to those in the prison house? Who were the prisoners?

The apostle Peter gives us the answer. Said he:

"For Christ also hath once suffered for sins, the just for the unjust, that he might bring us to God, being put to death in the flesh, but quickened by the Spirit: by which also he went and preached unto the spirits in prison; which sometime were disobedient, when once the longsuffering of God waited in the days of Noah, while the ark was a preparing, wherein few, that is, eight souls were saved by water." (1 Peter 3:18-20.)

Other Bible translations are very clear on this point. The spirits of those who were rebellious in the days of Noah and who died in the flood, in truth were held in a spirit prison in the hereafter. And Jesus did preach to the departed dead.

The Schoenfeld Authentic New Testament, for

example, says: "Christ himself died for sins once and for all, the just for the unjust, to bring us to God, being put to death in the flesh but revived in the spirit, in which also Enoch went and preached to the spirits in prison."

The New English Bible says, "And in the spirit he went and made his proclamation to the imprisoned spirits."

The Roman Catholic (Douay) Bible of 1947, giving essentially the same translation, adds in a footnote that Christ, after his death, "descended into the realm of the dead and brought them the Good Tidings; i.e. preached or proclaimed to them the Gospel."

So it is a scriptural fact that while his body lay in the tomb "until the third day," Christ, as an immortal spirit, went to the realm of departed spirits and there brought the gospel to the dead. And why?

Peter gives the answer: "For for this cause was the gospel preached also to them that are dead, that they might be judged according to men in the flesh, but live according to God in the spirit." (1 Peter 4:6.)

The Jerusalem Bible (Catholic) has this passage read: "And because he is their judge too, the dead had to be told the Good News as well, so that though, in their life on earth they had been through the judgement that comes to all humanity, they might come to God's life in the spirit."

The New English Bible reads: "Why was the Gospel preached to those who are dead? In order that, although in the body they received the sentence common to men, they might in the spirit be alive with the life of God."

The true understanding of it all was given in a vision to President Joseph F. Smith. On one occasion as he studied the scripture from Peter telling of the Lord's ministry among the dead, a vision burst upon him. First he saw the righteous dead, who knew the Savior was to visit them:

"I beheld that they were filled with joy and gladness, and were rejoicing together because the day of their deliverance was at hand. They were assembled awaiting the advent of the Son of God into the spirit world, to declare their redemption from the bands of death.

"Their sleeping dust was to be restored unto its perfect frame, bone to his bone, and the sinews and the flesh upon them, the spirit and the body to be united never again to be divided, that they might receive a fulness of joy.

"While this vast multitude waited and conversed, rejoicing in the hour of their deliverance from the chains of death, the Son of God appeared, declaring liberty to the captives who had been faithful; and there he preached to them the everlasting gospel, the doctrine of the resurrection and the redemption of mankind from the fall, and from individual sins on conditions of repentance.

"But unto the wicked he did not go, and among the ungodly and the unrepentant who had defiled themselves while in the flesh, his voice was not raised; neither did the rebellious who rejected the testimonies and the warnings of the ancient prophets behold his presence, nor look upon his face.

"Where these were, darkness reigned, but among the righteous there was peace; and the saints rejoiced in their redemption, and bowed the knee and acknowledged the Son of God as their Redeemer and Deliverer from death and the chains of hell. Their countenances shone, and the radiance from the presence of the Lord rested upon them, and they sang praises unto his holy name.

"I marveled, for I understood that the Savior spent about three years in his ministry among the Jews and those of the house of Israel, endeavoring to teach them the everlasting gospel and call them unto repentance; and yet, notwithstanding his mighty works, and miracles, and proclamation of the truth, in great power and authority, there were but few who hearkened to his voice, and rejoiced in his presence, and received salvation at his hands.

"But his ministry among those who were dead was limited to the brief time intervening between the crucifixion and his resurrection; and I wondered at the words of Peter wherein he said that the Son of God preached unto the spirits in prison, who sometime were disobedient, when once the long-suffering of God waited in the days of Noah—and how it was possible for him to preach to those spirits and perform the necessary labor among them in so short a time.

"And as I wondered, my eyes were opened, and my understanding quickened, and I perceived that the Lord went not in person among the wicked and the disobedient who had rejected the truth, to teach them; but behold, from among the righteous, he organized his forces and appointed messengers, clothed with power and authority, and commissioned them to go forth and carry the light of the gospel to them that were in darkness, even to all the spirits of men; and thus was the gospel preached to the dead.

"And the chosen messengers went forth to declare the acceptable day of the Lord and proclaim liberty to the captives who were bound, even unto all who would repent of their sins and receive the gospel.

"Thus was the gospel preached to those who had died in their sins, without a knowledge of the truth, or in transgression, having rejected the prophets.

"These were taught faith in God, repentance from sin, vicarious baptism for the remission of sins, the gift of the Holy Ghost by the laying on of hands, and all other principles of the gospel that were necessary for them to know in order to qualify themselves that they might be judged according to men in the flesh, but live according to God in the spirit.

"And so it was made known among the dead, both small and great, the unrighteous as well as the faithful, that redemption had been wrought through the sacrifice of the Son of God upon the cross.

"Thus was it made known that our Redeemer spent

his time during his sojourn in the world of spirits, instructing and preparing the faithful spirits of the prophets who had testified of him in the flesh; that they might carry the message of redemption unto all the dead, unto whom he could not go personally, because of their rebellion and transgression, that they through the ministration of his servants might also hear his words.'' (D&C 138:15-37. See also *Gospel Doctrine,* pp. 473–74.)

The Savior gave us this additional scripture in regard to the salvation of the dead:

''Verily, verily, I say unto you, The hour is coming, and now is, when the dead shall hear the voice of the Son of God: and they that hear shall live.

''For as the Father hath life in himself; so hath he given to the Son to have life in himself; and hath given him authority to execute judgment also, because he is the Son of man.

''Marvel not at this: for the hour is coming, in the which all that are in the graves shall hear his voice, and shall come forth; they that have done good, unto the resurrection of life; and they that have done evil, unto the resurrection of damnation.'' (John 5:25-29.)

With regard to the resurrection Isaiah declared: ''Thy dead men shall live, together with my dead body shall they arise.'' (Isaiah 26:19.)

Chapter Fourteen

ISAIAH'S SECOND CHAPTER

Let us now turn to Isaiah as he speaks of our day.

For Latter-day Saints, one of the most significant parts of the entire book of Isaiah is the second chapter. There Isaiah foretells the journey of the Saints to the Rocky Mountains and unfolds their ultimate destiny.

Micah gives the same prophecy, but in his own words. The modern Bible translations include both prophecies and in all cases confirm the meaning in the older versions. There can be no doubt that these prophecies refer strictly and specifically to the Latter-day Saints.

Isaiah speaks directly concerning the last days and uses that very expression. He said, "The mountain of the Lord's house shall be established in the top of the mountains." (Isaiah 2:2.) Scholars indicate that to the Jews, the expression "mountain of the Lord's house" simply meant the temple of God.

Before there were temples built on earth, the Lord sanctified places in the mountains and there instructed his prophets. Such places were regarded as being holy, and contributed to such expressions as the "temple of the mountain of the Lord" and "the mountain of the Lord's house." These were natural temples, in the open air, made sacred by the presence of God as he communed with his servants.

President Joseph Fielding Smith wrote:

"Of necessity the first sanctified temples were the mountain tops and secluded places in the wilderness. If we are correctly informed, Adam built his altar on a hill above the valley of Adam-ondi-Ahman. At that place the

Lord revealed to him the purpose of the fall and the mission of the Savior.

"Enoch stood in the place Mahujah. . . . Upon this mount Enoch beheld the heavens open, he was clothed upon by the glory of the Lord, he saw the Lord and spoke to him face to face. On this mount the Lord revealed to him the fulness of the plan of salvation. . . .

"It was upon the great mountain Shelem, which was sanctified and made holy, that the brother of Jared was commissioned and received one of the greatest revelations ever given unto man. . . .

"Jacob named the place where the Lord appeared to him, *Beth-el,* which interpreted means *the House of God. . . .*

"It was at the holy sanctuary on Horeb, called *the mountain of the Lord,* that Moses received his commission to deliver Israel. . . .

". . . These places became consecrated because there was no temple on the earth at that time. Joseph Smith prayed in the grove near his father's house, and that spot was made holy by the vision of the Father and the Son. . . .

"Shortly after the organization of the Church and when the membership was small, the Lord commanded the Saints to build a temple in which he could reveal the keys of authority and where the apostles could be endowed and prepared to prune his vineyard for the last time. . . .

"Had there been such a house when John the Baptist and Peter, James, and John came, they would have delivered their authority in it. Necessity made it expedient for them to come in the wilderness." (*Doctrines of Salvation,* Bookcraft, 1955, 2:232-34.)

And so it was that temple building began in these days. The fact that God required such structures is further seen in the glorious appearance that took place in the Kirtland Temple, when the Savior came, and various other personages, to restore keys of the kingdom of God.

It is also seen that at first mountain tops and the
wilderness were used instead of temples until such structures could be built. Hence temples became associated
with high mountains.

A temple will be built on Mount Zion in old Jerusalem
in the latter days. And, according to Isaiah, there will be
a temple also on the Mount Zion in the western world.
That holy house, he said, will be "exalted above the
hills" (Isaiah 2:2), that is, at some considerable altitude.

The structure that Isaiah saw, we are told by President Wilford Woodruff, is the Salt Lake Temple. In the
valley of the Great Salt Lake it stands at 4,300 feet above
sea level, with mountains ranging from 10,000 to nearly
12,000 feet in elevation surrounding the valley in which
the building stands.

When the Douay Bible (Roman Catholic) spoke of the
erection of that edifice, its translators used the expression "the house of the Lord shall be prepared" in the top
of the mountains.

"All nations shall flow unto it," that is, to the house
of the Lord thus built in the high mountain area. People
from "all nations" now do come to it, generally in three
categories.

One group is made up of tourists. An average of
nearly two million a year visit Temple Square in Salt
Lake City. That ten-acre parcel of land is one of the
greatest tourist attractions in the Mountain West. The
tourists sign registration slips at the visitors centers
showing that they represent countries from around the
world, including both sides of the Iron Curtain and both
sides of the "Bamboo" curtain. These tourists travel not
only to see Salt Lake City, but also to see the temple and
the Tabernacle and to hear the Tabernacle Choir and the
great organ.

Another group is composed of converts to the Church
from many lands who visit Church headquarters, the
General Authorities, and Temple Square. Many are from
areas where presently no temples exist, and hence they

enter the Salt Lake Temple to receive their blessings, which are given in various languages.

A third group is made up of those attending general conferences of the Church each spring and autumn. And who are they? They too are from "all nations." Many are lay members of the Church, but particularly some three thousand official delegates or representatives from Church units in about seventy nations are present to receive instructions. They include area administrators from the four quarters of the world, some two hundred regional representatives, also from many parts of the earth; stake presidents, high councilors, bishoprics, patriarchs, and auxiliary leaders. They are local officers living in many lands.

They, of course, speak various languages. Translations of all sermons are given in about thirty different tongues. A large room in the Tabernacle houses the translators, each one working in his own language, having his or her own desk with the necessary privacy to allow for full concentration on the message being given.

It is an inspiration to see these translators and how they work. They do so prayerfully, constantly seeking the inspiration of the Lord to guide them in transmitting the messages of the General Authorities to their own people in their own languages. Simultaneous translations are provided for the visiting officials from overseas who are in the congregation. But beyond that, the translations are sent abroad to local members in other nations by telephone, cable, and satellite. Video tapes are also made in various languages, and are sent to still other nations for subsequent release in local chapels.

The prophecies of Isaiah and Micah are literally fulfilled in these activities. Officials from other lands who come to the conference in Salt Lake City are delegates or representatives of congregations in their homelands, thus "flowing" from these nations. When they return to their homes, they make reports on the conference to their people.

With present technical advancements, conference proceedings by cable, satellite, and video tape are now made available to most free nations on earth. Members who cannot travel to Utah listen with great attention to the reports thus provided, and in this way, such congregations also "flow unto it" in spirit if not in the flesh.

That both Isaiah and Micah meant these Church members who come to hear and obey the words of the Lord is evident from these words: "Many people shall go and say, Come ye, and let us go up to the mountain [temple] of the Lord, to the house of the God of Jacob; *and he will teach us of his ways, and we will walk in his paths.*" (Isaiah 2:3. Italics added.)

That is exactly what happens at each general conference. The Saints do assemble from the many nations, they do gather to learn, they are taught, and they do obey, literally walking "in his paths."

It is all a great miracle. It is a remarkable fulfillment of prophecy.

Isaiah indicates, as further evidence of this being in the latter days, that afterward God "shall judge among the nations, and shall rebuke many people: and they shall beat their swords into plowshares, and their spears into pruning hooks: nation shall not lift up sword against nation, neither shall they learn war any more." (Isaiah 2:4.)

This obviously refers to the opening of the millennial reign of the Savior. The coming of the Saints to the Rocky Mountains was definitely preliminary to that blessed period.

"O house of Jacob," comes Isaiah's invitation, "come ye, and let us walk in the light of the Lord." (Verse 5.) One of the most important parts of that prophecy, however, we should now mention: "For out of Zion shall go forth the law, and the word of the Lord from Jerusalem." (Verse 3.)

All of America is Zion, according to the Prophet Joseph Smith, but there will be two central places in America from which the law of the Lord will go.

The first is Salt Lake City, the headquarters of the Church until such time as the New Jerusalem is built. We speak of Salt Lake City as Zion in this sense. It is the Zion high in the Rocky Mountains.

Certainly from there the law of the Lord is going abroad to the nations right now. It is in Utah that most of the missionaries are trained before going abroad. From there instructions go to stakes and missions the world around. It is to Temple Square that the congregations assemble at each general conference to be taught the law and the word of the Lord.

But the great Zion of the Lord—the New Jerusalem—from which the Lord will reign through the millennium will be built in Jackson County, Missouri, the center for the Lord's greatest modern temple. As the Savior reigns for a thousand years, accompanied by his Saints, he most assuredly will issue his laws and directions to all the world from that great center.

But what of the other Jerusalem from which the word of the Lord will issue also? It will be the Old Jerusalem in Palestine, restored. A great temple is to be built there also. The Tribes of Israel will gather there, fulfilling the mighty prophecies concerning their eventual happiness.

America is the land of Joseph, and the tribes of Ephraim and Manasseh, sons of Joseph, will inherit this land, with the great New Jerusalem as their capital city. Palestine will be headquarters for the other tribes, centering in the restored Old Jerusalem.

Of the American Zion, the Lord says this:

"And it shall be called the New Jerusalem, a land of peace, a city of refuge, a place of safety for the saints of the Most High God; and the glory of the Lord shall be there, and the terror of the Lord also shall be there, insomuch that the wicked will not come unto it, and it shall be called Zion.

"And it shall come to pass among the wicked, that every man that will not take his sword against his neighbor must flee unto Zion for safety. And there shall be gathered unto it out of every nation under heaven; and it shall be the only people that shall not be at war one with another.

"And it shall be said among the wicked: Let us not go up to battle against Zion, for the inhabitants of Zion are terrible; wherefore we cannot stand.

"And it shall come to pass that the righteous shall be gathered out from among all nations, and shall come to Zion, singing with songs of everlasting joy." (D&C 45:66-71.)

Chapter Fifteen

WHAT ISAIAH SAW

The Salt Lake Temple is the edifice that Isaiah saw, high in the mountains, the holy place to which all nations should flow, where "he will teach us of his ways, and we will walk in his paths." (Isaiah 2:3.)

This is the firm declaration of President Wilford Woodruff. He also said that the Salt Lake Tabernacle was a part of the fulfillment of Isaiah's words. Following is an excerpt from a sermon that he gave:

Today I stand in a tabernacle filled with some twelve thousand of the Latter-day Saints who have followed the pioneers into these valleys of the mountains.

When we cast our eyes over these valleys, then a desert, today they are teeming with the industry of one hundred and fifty thousand of the sons and daughters of Zion, who have been gathered by the commandments of God and the proclamation of the Gospel of Christ.

We, as pioneers and as the people of God, are fulfilling prophecy and making history. This tabernacle in which we are today, is the very tabernacle that Isaiah saw in vision twenty-six hundred years ago, that should be as a shadow in the daytime from the heat, and a covert from the storm and from the rain.

We are also building the temple of our God, on this block, which the prophet saw was to be built in the last days upon the mountain of the Lord's house, and be established on the tops of the mountains for all men to flow unto.

"And many people shall go and say, Come ye and let us go up to the mountain of the Lord, to the house of the God of Jacob; and He will teach us of His ways and we will walk in His paths; for out of Zion shall go forth the law, and the word of the Lord from Jerusalem."

Our whole life, history and travels have been pointed out by the ancient prophets. As the pioneers came into this barren desert and the Saints have followed them to fulfill the prophecies, to make the desert blossom as the rose, to sow our grain beside all small streams and still waters, and use the fir, the pine and the box, to beautify the place of God's sanctuary and to make the place of His feet glorious, and as there is but a remnant of us left as pioneers, or Battalion, or Zion's Camp, let us magnify our calling and build up the Zion and Kingdom of God until it is perfected before the heavens and the earth, and not disappoint those who sent us, nor those who have seen us by vision and revelation, but let us finish and fulfill our destiny to the satisfaction of our heavenly Father, His angels and all good men. (*Elders' Journal* 4:130.)

In his prayer dedicating the Salt Lake Temple, President Woodruff used these words further indicating that he regarded the Salt Lake Temple as the one foretold by Isaiah:

O Lord, we regard with intense and indescribable feelings the completion of this sacred house. Deign to accept this the fourth temple which thy covenant children have been assisted by thee in erecting in these mountains.

In past ages thou didst inspire with thy Holy Spirit thy servants, the Prophets, to speak of a time in the latter days when the mountain of the Lord's house should be established in the top of the mountains, and should be exalted above the hills.

We thank thee that we have had the glorious opportunity of contributing to the fulfillment of these visions of thine ancient seers, and that thou hast condescended to permit us to take part in the great work.

And as this portion of thy servant's words has thus so marvelously been brought to pass, we pray thee, with increased faith and renewed hope, that all their words with regard to thy great work in gathering thine Israel and building up thy kingdom on earth in the last days may be as amply fulfilled, and that, O Lord, speedily.

We come before thee with joy and thanksgiving, with spirits jubilant and hearts filled with praise, that thou hast permitted us to see this day for which, during these forty years, we have hoped, and toiled, and prayed, when we can dedicate unto thee this house which we have built to thy most glorious name.

One year ago we set the capstone with shouts of Hosanna to God and the Lamb. And to-day we dedicate the whole unto thee, with all that pertains unto it, that it may be holy in thy sight; that it may be a house of prayer, a house of praise and of worship; that thy glory may rest upon it; that thy holy presence may be continually in it; that it may be the abode of thy Well-Beloved Son, our Savior; that the angels who stand before thy face may be the hallowed messengers who shall visit it, bearing to us thy wishes and thy will, that it may be sanctified and consecrated in all its parts holy unto thee, the God of Israel, the Almighty Ruler of mankind. (*Millennial Star* 55:334-35.)

President Brigham Young was shown the Salt Lake Temple in vision and the pattern by which it was to be built. Said he:

I scarcely ever say much about revelations, or visions, but suffice it to say, five years ago last July I was here, and saw in the spirit the temple not ten feet from where we have laid the chief cornerstone. I have not inquired what kind of a temple we should build. Why? Because it was represented before me. I have never looked upon that ground, but the vision of it was there. I see it as plainly as if it was in reality before me. Wait until it is done. I will say, however, that it will have six towers, to begin with, instead of one. (*Discourses of Brigham Young,* Deseret Book, 1977, p. 410.)

At another time President Young said: "I want this temple that we are now building to the name of our God, to stand for all time to come as a monument of the industry, faithfulness, faith, and integrity of the Latter-day Saints who were driven into the mountains." (Ibid., p. 411.)

President Young indicated that the Lord gave the pattern of the Kirtland Temple to the Prophet Joseph Smith: "The Church, through our beloved Prophet Joseph, was commanded to build a temple to the Most High, in Kirtland, Ohio. Joseph not only received revelation and commandment to build a temple, but he received a pattern also, as did Moses for the tabernacle, and Solomon for his temple; for without a pattern, he could not know what was wanted, having never seen one, and not having experienced its use." (Ibid., p. 415.)

President Young indicated that the Prophet Joseph received the pattern for the Nauvoo Temple by revelation. Such divine direction was needed, of course, because this temple was different from that in Kirtland. It had specific uses unknown to Joseph Smith until new revelation came.

All of the temples built by the pioneer Latter-day Saints were constructed at great sacrifice because of the poverty of the people. The Saints knew the importance of obtaining the ordinances of salvation, and therefore gave temple building as great emphasis as they did missionary work.

In speaking of the completion of the Salt Lake Temple, the *Elders' Journal* editorialized: "The edifice completed stands on this block [Temple Square]. It speaks for itself. It is located in the top of the mountains. It is exalted above the hills and people from all nations have come unto it. Thus the specifications laid down by the prophet of old are satisfied, his prophecy fulfilled." (*Elders' Journal* 24:148.)

When the temple was completed and dedicated by President Woodruff in 1893, of course, all nations had not yet begun to "flow unto it." But today Temple Square is one of the chief tourist attractions of the Mountain West.

Year after year it exceeds or equals the patronage of most of the national and state parks of the area. Visitors at Temple Square each year rival even the number who go to Yellowstone Park.

They come as tourists; they come to conventions; they come for business; and they come to learn about genealogy. Two successful World Conferences on Records have been held in Salt Lake City, in 1969 and in 1980, in which several hundred researchers and archivists from various lands conducted classes and gave instruction to the thousands who attended.

Response to the 1980 World Conference on Records was outstanding. For example, Lord Teviot from London summed up his feelings—and the feelings of others—concerning the conference when he responded to queries from the press: "Absolutely marvelous! There isn't another genealogical or personal or family conference in the world that can compare with the World Conference on Records."

Approximately 11,500 admission badges were issued.

Participants from thirty nations attended the conference, including individuals from India, Thailand, Indonesia, mainland China, Taiwan, Japan, Tunisia, Kenya, Israel, Yugoslavia, and South Africa. Approximately 2,000 registrants were not members of the Church; 6,600 registrants were from Utah, and 500 were from outside the United States.

Hundreds of thousands of tourists and other visitors come to our temples and visitors centers situated in the "tops of the mountains." These visitors literally come from "all nations." It is to be remembered that they not only come to the tops of the mountains as tourists, they come to see the temples! These many visitors are truly a living fulfillment of Isaiah's mighty prophecy.

One of the most remarkable things about Isaiah's prophecies as they relate to America was explained by the Savior himself as he ministered among the Nephites.

The Lord was discussing the role of the Gentiles in America in the latter days and said: "If the Gentiles will repent and return unto me, saith the Father, behold they shall be numbered among my people, O house of Israel."

Then he added these significant words, as we keep in mind that the land of which he spoke was America:

"Verily, verily, I say unto you, thus hath the Father commanded me—that I should give *unto this people this land for their inheritance.*

"And then the words of the prophet Isaiah shall be fulfilled, which say: Thy watchmen shall lift up the voice; with the voice together shall they sing, for they shall see eye to eye when the Lord shall bring again Zion.

"Break forth into joy, sing together, ye waste places of Jerusalem; for the Lord hath comforted his people, he hath redeemed Jerusalem. The Lord hath made bare his holy arm in the eye of all the nations; and all the ends of the earth shall see the salvation of God." (3 Nephi 16:13, 16-20. See also Isaiah 52:8-10.)

Isaiah truly spoke of America. Is it any wonder, then, that the latter-day temple that he saw in the tops of the mountains was truly an American temple, built in the Rockies, the highest mountains on this continent?

Chapter Sixteen

TEMPLE HILL

Isaiah and Micah were contemporaries, and both dealt with the constant problems in the nation of Judah. Both made similar predictions, and did so especially and specifically with respect to the mountain of the Lord's house in latter days.

The Knox Translation (Roman Catholic) of Micah's words is of particular interest. They appear in the 1955 version of their Bible, published in Great Britain under the imprimatur of Archbishop Griffin of Westminster. The translation of this passage reads:

"The Temple hill! One day it shall stand there, highest of all the mountain-heights, overtopping the peaks of them, and the nations will flock there together.

"A multitude of peoples will make their way to it, crying, Come, let us climb up to the Lord's mountain-peak, to the house where the God of Jacob dwells; he shall teach us the right way, we will walk in the paths he has chosen.

"The Lord's command shall go out of Sion, his word from Jerusalem; over thronging peoples he shall sit in judgment, give award to great nations far away. Sword they will fashion into ploughshare and spear into pruning hook, no room there shall be for nation to levy war against nation and train itself in arms." (Michaeas 4:1-3.)

Another Catholic Bible, the Jerusalem Bible, has the passage from Isaiah read like this: "In the days to come the mountain of the Temple of Yahweh [Jehovah] shall tower above the mountains and be lifted higher than the hills. All the nations will stream to it, peoples without number will come to it; and they will say: 'Come, let us go up to the mountain of Yahweh, to the Temple of the God of Jacob that he may teach us his ways so that we may walk in his paths." (Isaiah 2:3.)

The version of Micah given in this same Bible reads: "In the days to come the mountain of the Temple of Yahweh will be put on top of the mountains and be lifted higher than the hills. The peoples will stream to it, nations without number will come to it; and they will say, 'Come, let us go up to the mountain of Yahweh, to the Temple of the God of Jacob so that he may teach us his ways and we may walk in his paths."

In the New World Translation these words are used: "The mountain of the house of Jehovah will become firmly established above the top of the mountains." (Micah 4:1.)

The King James Version of Isaiah reads on this point:

"And it shall come to pass in the last days, that the mountain of the Lord's house shall be established in the top of the mountains, and shall be exalted above the hills; and all nations shall flow unto it.

"And many people shall go and say, Come ye, and let us go up to the mountain of the Lord, to the house of the God of Jacob; and he will teach us of his ways, and we will walk in his paths: for out of Zion shall go forth the law, and the word of the Lord from Jerusalem.

"And he shall judge among the nations, and shall rebuke many people: and they shall beat their swords into plowshares, and their spears into pruninghooks: nation shall not lift up sword against nation, neither shall they learn war any more.

"O house of Jacob, come ye, and let us walk in the light of the Lord." (Isaiah 2:2-5.)

Micah's prediction was discussed by the late Elder Orson Pratt of the Council of the Twelve. He began by asking this question:

Why is Zion commanded to *"get up into the high mountains?"* Why did He exclaim so emphatically, "O Zion, that bringest good tidings, get thee up into the high mountains!"

Surely He must have seen some cause of an important nature, why Zion should go into a high mountain, or He never would have uttered a commandment to take effect nearly three thousand years in the future.

One of the principal causes why Zion should be required to "get up into a high mountain" is, that they might build a house of God there, in fulfillment of prophecy.

Micah, (chap. 4), says: "But in the last days it shall come to pass that the mountain of the house of the Lord shall be established in the tops of the mountains, and it shall be exalted above the hills; and people shall flow unto it.

"And many nations shall say, come and let us go up to the mountain of the Lord, and to the house of the God of Jacob; and He will teach us of His ways, and we will walk in His paths, for the law shall go forth of Zion, and the word of the Lord from Jerusalem." . . . All this was to take place in the "last days."

We can see the propriety then of Isaiah's calling upon the people of the latter-day Zion to "get up into the high mountain." For it is there that the "house of the God of Jacob" is to be built. It is from the *mountains* that Zion shall send forth her perfect law to teach the kings of the earth wisdom, and the nations afar off a perfect order of government.

It is in the house of God which shall be in the *mountains,* that "many nations" shall be taught in the ways of the Lord, and be instructed to "walk in his paths."

There must be something connected with the House of God in the mountains which is very peculiar, or it would never excite the attention of many nations.

There are many thousands of houses built up at the present day, professing to be the houses of God. Scores of them are to be seen in almost every city of America and Europe; yet there does not appear anything very striking in any of them.

There is not one house among the whole of them that has excited the attention of even *one* nation. There is a very good reason for this; for all nations have been entirely destitute of a "house of God" for more than seventeen hundred years. Indeed, the house of God was not to be built again until the *last days;* and, when it was built, it should be built in the *mountains,* and not in several hundred places among the nations.

The "house of God" could not be built without new revelation to give the pattern of its various apartments. Without new revelation Zion would not know the precise time to "get up into the high mountains," they would not know the precise mountain where God would have His house to be built.

The "house of God" never was in any past age, and never can

be in any future age, built without express commandments or new revelations being given to the people who built it.

When the house of God shall be built in the right time, and in the right place, and according to the right pattern, and by the right people, then it will be acknowledged by the God of Jacob—then His glory shall rest upon it, and His presence shall come into it. . . .

Then *"many nations"* shall say, come, let us go up to Zion, for God is there; His house is there; His people are there; His law is there; His glory and power are there; the "perfection of beauty" is there; whatsoever is great, and good, and noble are there.

Come, then, let us go up, "for he will teach us of his ways, and we will walk in his paths," and we will no more lift up our swords against nations, but convert them into the peaceful implements of husbandry, and henceforth dwell with the people of God.

It is to accomplish this great, this marvellous, this wonderful work, that Zion in the *last days* is commanded to *"get up into the high mountain."*

Thousands of her noble enterprising sons have already traversed the widely extended plains of North America, and have ascended the great central range of mountains that form as it were, the backbone of that continent, and among its deep, retired, and lonely recesses they have *"sought out"* a resting place for the children of Zion. . . .

In the latter part of July we arrived in the valley, called by us the "valley of the Great Salt Lake," here we located a site for a city, called by us "Great Salt Lake City."

In this city we reserved a block for the building of a house unto the God of Jacob; this we called *"Temple Block."* . . .

Well might the ancient prophets speak of Zion going up into the high mountains, and of the house of the God of Jacob being built in the mountains, when it is ascertained that the "Temple Block" is 4300 feet above the level of the ocean.

It cannot, for a moment, be supposed that Zion would go up to the top of some mountain peak, and undertake to build a city and a temple upon its snowy summit.

But the word mountain in those passages doubtless means some high elevated portion of the earth, and yet not so high as to be rendered sterile by eternal frosts and snows, for this would unfit it for the habitation of man. . . .

The latter-day Zion was not to be built where Zion anciently stood, that is, in Jerusalem, the place of which has been well known for ages; but in the "high mountain," in a place unknown, that should be "sought out;" and there they should be called, "the holy people"—"the redeemed of the Lord"—"a city not forsaken."

This was something, too, that was to take place in connection with the great preparatory work for the coming of the Lord: for it will be seen in the above passage that the "end of the world" was about this time to hear a proclamation concerning His coming, "His reward being with him, and His work before Him."

How beautiful upon the mountains are the feet of those who are publishing "good tidings," that are saying unto Zion, "behold, thy God reigneth."

Let the servants of the Lord cry aloud to the children of Zion scattered abroad, saying: Go ye "up into the high mountain" and build yourselves a city, and the God of Jacob a house; for "He will suddenly come to His temple," and reign in Mount Zion, and in Jerusalem, and before His ancients gloriously. (*Contributor* 12:307-10.)

Chapter Seventeen

OUR HYMN OF PRAISE

One of the best-loved hymns of the Latter-day Saints memorializes the successful fulfillment of Isaiah's prophecy foretelling the journey of the Saints to the tops of the mountains. It is "High on the Mountain Top," written by Joel H. Johnson with the music by Ebenezer Beesley.

The hymn tells of the banner of Israel being unfurled high in the mountains, where the temple of God will be reared, "his glory to display," and where we shall be taught his word.

The entire hymn reads as follows:

High on the mountain top
A banner is unfurled;
Ye nations, now look up;
It waves to all the world;
In Deseret's sweet, peaceful land—
On Zion's mount behold it stand!

For God remembers still
His promise made of old
That he on Zion's hill
Truth's standard would unfold!
Her light should there attract the gaze
Of all the world in latter days.

His house shall there be reared
His glory to display;
And people shall be heard
In distant lands to say,
We'll now go up and serve the Lord,
Obey his truth and learn his word.

For there we shall be taught
The law that will go forth,
With truth and wisdom fraught,
To govern all the earth;
Forever there his ways we'll tread,
And save ourselves with all our dead.

Then hail to Deseret!
A refuge for the good,
And safety for the great,
If they but understood
That God with plagues will shake the world
Till all its thrones shall down be hurled.

In Deseret doth truth
Rear up its royal head;
Though nations may oppose,
Still wider it shall spread;
Yes, truth and justice, love and grace,
In Deseret find ample place.

—Hymns, **No. 62**

Chapter Eighteen

WHY BUILD TEMPLES?

The Latter-day Saints are unique in the world in many ways, and one of them is in the construction of temples. There are many structures in many lands that mankind regard as temples. But the temples of the Latter-day Saints are different. They are built after a revealed pattern, and in them are given saving ordinances of the gospel for the living and the dead.

The Latter-day Saints have been commanded to build temples just as Solomon was commanded to build a temple, and Moses was commanded to carry a portable "temple" or tabernacle in the wilderness as the tribes wandered for forty years. In temples, and only in them, are sacred ordinances provided that are restricted by the Lord to such sacred places.

In our day, there are two general categories of ordinances in the gospel: those that may be administered outside a temple and those that are given only in a temple.

Those permitted outside the temple include baptism of new members, confirmation, the bestowal of the gift of the Holy Ghost, and ordination to the priesthood.

But what are those ordinances that are so sacred that they may be given only inside a temple? They are called endowments and sealings, and they have special significance. They are given to the living, but vicariously for the dead also. Work for the dead is one of the greatest uses of the temples.

The late Elder John A. Widtsoe of the Council of the Twelve explained these ordinances and the symbolism attached to them. He wrote as follows:

In God's kingdom are many gradations, which lead to exaltation. . . . Those who hunger and thirst for righteousness and labor for the fulfillment of the promise involved in the gift of the Holy Ghost will advance farther than those who placidly sit by with no driving desire within them. Temple worship is an avenue to exaltation in God's kingdom.

God's definition of a temple is given over and over again in . . . the Doctrine and Covenants. A temple is a place in which those whom he has chosen are endowed with power from on high.

And what is power? Knowledge made alive and useful—that is intelligence; and intelligence in action—that is power.

Our temples give us power—a power based on enlarged knowledge and intelligence—a power from on high, of a quality with God's own power. . . .

Sealings, for time and eternity, have the purpose of tying together father and son, mother and daughter, the living and the dead, from age to age. In addition it emphasizes the authority of the priesthood. . . .

When man contemplates the full meaning of the sealing ordinance . . . he is overwhelmed with the boundless power that it implies and the weight of authority that it represents. . . .

In the wonderful Section 124, of the Doctrine and Covenants, the Lord has described the work to be done in the temples, including the holy endowment:

"For a baptismal font there is not upon the earth, that they, my Saints, may be baptized for those who are dead. . . .

"For therein are the keys of the Holy Priesthood, ordained that you may receive honor and glory. . . .

"And again, verily I say unto you, How shall your washings be acceptable unto me, except ye perform them in a house which you have built to my name?

"For, for this cause I commanded Moses that he should build a tabernacle, that they should bear it with them in the wilderness, and to build a house in the land of promise, that those ordinances might be revealed which had been hid from before the world was;

"Therefore, verily I say unto you, that your anointings, and your washings, and your baptisms for the dead, and your solemn assemblies, and your memorials for your sacrifices, by the sons of Levi, and for your oracles in your most holy places, wherein you receive conversations, and your statutes and judgments, for the beginning of the revelations and foundation of Zion, and for the glory, honor, and endowment of all her municipals, are ordained by the ordinance of my holy house which my people are always commanded to build unto my holy name."

At first reading the full meaning may not be clear, yet in these few verses lie the germs of practically everything that belongs to or is done in the house of the Lord.

Dr. James E. Talmage, under authority of the Church, has also discussed the meaning of the endowment, in the book called "The House of the Lord." I quote a part of it.

"The Temple Endowment, as administered in modern temples, comprises instruction relating to the significance and sequence of past dispensations, and the importance of the present as the greatest and grandest era in human history. This course of instruction includes a recital of the most prominent events of the creative period, the condition of our first parents in the Garden of Eden, their disobedience and consequent expulsion from that blissful abode, their condition in the lone and dreary world when doomed to live by labor and sweat, the plan of redemption by which the great transgression may be atoned, the restoration of the Gospel with all its ancient powers and privileges, the absolute and indispensable condition of personal purity and devotion to the right in present life, and a strict compliance with Gospel requirements.

"As will be shown, the temples erected by the Latter-day Saints provide for the giving of these instructions in separate rooms, each devoted to a particular part of the course; and by this provision it is possible to have several classes under instruction at one time.

"The ordinances of the endowment embody certain obligations on the part of the individual, such as covenant and promise to observe the law of strict virtue and chastity, to be charitable, benevolent, tolerant and pure; to devote both talent and material means to the spread of truth and the uplifting of the race; to maintain devotion to the cause of truth; and to seek in every way to contribute to the great preparation that the earth may be made ready to receive her King,—the Lord Jesus Christ. With the taking of each covenant and the assuming of each obligation of a promised blessing is pronounced, contingent upon the faithful observance of the conditions.

"No jot, iota, or tittle of the temple rites is otherwise than uplifting and sanctifying. In every detail the endowment ceremony contributes to covenants of morality of life, consecration of person to high ideals, devotion to truth, patriotism to nation and allegiance to God. The blessings of the House of the Lord are restricted to no privileged class; every member of the Church may have admission to the temple with the right to participate in the ordinances thereof, if he comes duly accredited as of worthy life and conduct." [*The House of the Lord*, pp. 83–84.]

In no part of the temple service is the spirit or the purpose of the temple worship so completely shown as in the endowment. . . .

The holy endowment is deeply symbolic. "Going through the temple" is not a very good phrase; for temple worship implies a great effort of mind and concentration if we are to understand the mighty symbols that pass in review before us.

Everything must be arranged to attune our hearts, our minds, and our souls to the work. Everything about us must contribute to the peace of mind that enables us to study and to understand the mysteries, if you choose, that are unfolded before us. . . .

Some have gone through the temple looking at the outward form and not the inner meaning of things. The form of the endowment is of earthly nature, but it *symbolizes great spiritual truths.*

All that we do on this earth is earthly, but all is symbolic of great spiritual truths. To build this temple, earth had to be dug; wood had to be cut; stone was quarried and brought down the canyon.

It was dusty and dirty work, and made us sweat—it was of this earth—yet it was the necessary preparation for the mighty spiritual ordinances that are carried on daily in this magnificent temple.

The endowment itself is symbolic; it is a series of symbols of vast realities, too vast for full understanding. . . .

This brings me to a few words concerning symbolism. We live in a world of symbols. We know nothing, except by symbols. We make a few marks on a sheet of paper, and we say that they form a word which stands for love, or hate, or charity, or God or eternity. The marks may not be very beautiful to the eye. No one finds fault with the symbols on the pages of a book because they are not as mighty in their own beauty as the things which they represent. We do not quarrel with the symbol "G-o-d" because it is not very beautiful, yet represents the majesty of God.

We are glad to have symbols, if only the meaning of the symbols is brought home to us. . . .

We live in a world of symbols. *No man or woman can come out of the temple endowed as he should be, unless he has seen, beyond the symbol, the mighty realities for which the symbols stand.* ("Temple Worship," in *Utah Genealogical and Historical Magazine* 12:50-64.)

Chapter Nineteen

THE MARVELOUS WORK

The Book of Mormon is our finest key to an understanding of Isaiah. Not even Jewish scholarship can approach it in revealing what the prophet's words really mean. To understand his work requires an acceptance of the restoration of the gospel, for that is the subject of much of his writing.

It is admitted that many parts of Isaiah are difficult to comprehend, but a great deal is made clear by extensive passages in the Book of Mormon, which include explanations by ancient American prophets who loved Isaiah, studied his writings, preached from them, and interpreted them.

One of the outstanding examples of this phenomenon relates to chapter 29 of Isaiah, where the prophet foretells the publication of the Book of Mormon and speaks of the Prophet Joseph Smith as an unlearned man, which he was at the time referred to, but through whom the Lord accomplished a marvelous work and a wonder.

Isaiah's writing on this subject is one of the great testimonies for Latter-day Saints concerning the restoration of the gospel. It is verily true that Isaiah saw our day and described much of our work in considerable detail.

Let us examine Isaiah 29 and then turn to chapters 27 and 28 in Second Nephi wherein is laid before us in beautiful clarity an understanding of this matter.

Isaiah begins his passages by mentioning a city known as Ariel. He identifies it as the "city where David dwelt," which, of course, is Jerusalem. He mentions the woes of Ariel, since the people of that ancient city had become apostate, turning as they did to idolatry.

Then he speaks of a nation that he says shall be "as Ariel" in that it also would be in deep trouble because of apostasy. Hence it would fall to the dust and be destroyed suddenly.

We know from Book of Mormon writings that this other nation was indeed "as Ariel" in many respects. It was the Nephite nation. It belonged to the House of Israel, as did the Jews. It had inspired prophets, as did the Jews. It had the same scriptures as were possessed by the Jews, the entire Bible from Moses to Jeremiah.

The Lord blessed the Nephites when they were obedient, just as he did the Jews, but he left them to suffer when they disobeyed him, also as he did the Jews.

This branch of the House of Israel, which was "as Ariel," had been led from Palestine to the Western Hemisphere by the Lord. From them sprang the Nephites, who eventually apostatized to the extent that the Lord allowed them to be destroyed in a dreadful war with the Lamanites in which but one man was left to tell the tale.

Isaiah's description of the Nephites in no way reflects the lives or activities of the Jews. The Jews were not destroyed. They survived captivity and are still with us. It is estimated that they now number 16 million in the world altogether. There are about 3 million in Palestine and some 6 million in the United States. So obviously they were not destroyed suddenly or otherwise. Neither was the city of Jerusalem ever destroyed. It suffered repeated invasions and plunderings, but it still stands today, a bone of contention between Jews and Arabs.

Isaiah's words describe the New World branch of the House of Israel to perfection.

The Jews did not bury their scriptures in the ground to come forth in the latter days. They carefully preserved them and still read them in the synagogues. But the ancient Nephites buried many of their records in the ground for safekeeping, just as did other early peoples. Numerous such instances have been brought to light in various lands by archaeologists.

The Nephite branch of the House of Israel prepared records with great care, engraving some of them in stone and others in metal. Those in metal were buried in the ground in box-like stone containers.

Isaiah saw that an ancient record would come out of the ground, literally, whereby the nation described "as Ariel" would deliver an important message to the modern world.

Isaiah said these people would "speak out of the ground, and [their] speech shall be low out of the dust, and [their] voice shall be as of one that hath a familiar spirit, out of the ground, and [their] speech shall whisper out of the dust." (Isaiah 29:4.)

In this one passage Isaiah tells us four times that the message should come out of the ground and out of the dust. Did he not earnestly try to make this clear? Did he not understand the importance of repetition in teaching this great fact? So *four times* he declared that this record would come out of the ground, out of the dust. That was a major part of the identification of that record and needed emphasis. Could Isaiah have been more explicit?

At no time did Ariel, or Jerusalem, ever speak "out of the dust" in this manner. Never was a Jewish record buried and brought forth in such a way that the speech of an entire people came out of the ground.

Some might point to the Dead Sea Scrolls as evidence that certain Jewish records did come out of the ground. It is acknowledged that these scrolls came from caves, but they did not represent the Jewish nation as such. They came only from a small detached apostate cult that had separated itself from the main body of Jews and were known as separatists. Let it be noted that there was nothing new about the writings on those scrolls. *The Jews already had the books thus found,* and in a much better state of preservation than anything that came out of Qumran. So the Dead Sea Scrolls could in no way be related to the prophecy of Isaiah.

The whole nation that was likened "as Ariel" literally was destroyed suddenly, leaving only one man to survive. It was he who buried their final record in the ground, to be brought forth in these last days, as Isaiah saw.

That record has a vital message for Jews and Gentiles, for Chicanos, for Native Americans, Polynesians, and anyone else who will read it. It testifies of Christ! It is a second witness of the Redeemer! It is on a footing equal to the Bible! It is the Book of Mormon!

Isaiah makes it clear that this "speech out of the ground" would be in the form of a book. This is another factor that disqualifies the Dead Sea Scrolls from consideration with this prophecy.

Particular and very peculiar circumstances were to surround the coming forth of this book, says Isaiah. It would be given for publication to an *unlearned man,* a most unusual thing. What a specific and extraordinary stipulation the prophet makes! But it is vital to the proper identification of the record.

Isaiah also declares that some of the words of the book—but not the book itself—would be given to a learned man who would reject those words, since they came from a "sealed" book that he had never seen. That the book itself would be given to an unlearned man is quite an unusual circumstance. It is also a highly significant part of the identification of the ancient record.

None of these factors can possibly relate to the Qumran scrolls, but they definitely do narrow the identification of the book of which Isaiah spoke, and to a very fine point indeed.

The prophet Isaiah further said that pursuant to the publication of the book, the Lord would perform a "marvelous work and a wonder" that would baffle the wise and prudent men of the earth. The Qumran scrolls were not involved in any such occurrence.

One of the striking things about Isaiah's prediction is that the time of its fulfillment is specified. It was destined to happen just "a little while" before Palestine would again become fruitful, just before the restoration of the Holy Land in these modern times.

Now let us read Isaiah's words:

"And the vision of all is become unto you as the words of a book that is sealed, which men deliver to one that is learned, saying, Read this, I pray thee: and he saith, I cannot; for it is sealed:

"And the book is delivered to him that is not learned, saying, Read this, I pray thee: and he saith, I am not learned.

"Wherefore the Lord said, Forasmuch as this people draw near me with their mouth, and with their lips do honour me, but have removed their heart far from me, and their fear toward me is taught by the precept of men:

"Therefore, behold, I will proceed to do a marvellous work among this people, even a marvellous work and a wonder: for the wisdom of their wise men shall perish, and the understanding of their prudent men shall be hid. . . .

"Is it not yet a very little while, and Lebanon shall be turned into a fruitful field, and the fruitful field shall be esteemed as a forest?

"And in that day shall the deaf hear the words of the book, and the eyes of the blind shall see out of obscurity, and out of darkness.

"The meek also shall increase their joy in the Lord, and the poor among men shall rejoice in the Holy One of Israel." (Isaiah 29:11-14, 17-19.)

Who can understand these puzzling words? Only the Latter-day Saints, and then only through the use of the Book of Mormon. To the worldly wise, these words form one of the deep mysteries of the Holy Scriptures. But they are plain to those whom God chooses to bring about his "strange" task (Isaiah 28:21), his "marvellous work and a wonder."

Chapter Twenty

NEPHI'S EXPLANATION

Nephi is the author of the description of these important events as they are recorded in the Book of Mormon. He did more than merely outline or repeat what Isaiah said in his brief account. He provided a rich abundance of additional information, including the fact that part of the book was sealed and was not to be opened at this time. It is obvious that this fact could not be related to the Qumran scrolls either.

The sealed portion, Nephi said, contained an account of events foreseen in prophecy from the beginning to the end of the world.

The "unlearned man" was forbidden to touch the sealed portion, but was instructed to translate and publish that part which was not sealed. Nephi said:

"For behold, the Lord hath poured out upon you the spirit of deep sleep. For behold, ye have closed your eyes, and ye have rejected the prophets; and your rulers, and the seers hath he covered because of your iniquity.

"And it shall come to pass that the Lord God shall bring forth unto you the words of a book, and they shall be the words of them which have slumbered.

"And behold the book shall be sealed; and in the book shall be a revelation from God, from the beginning of the world to the ending thereof.

"Wherefore, because of the things which are sealed up, the things which are sealed shall not be delivered in the day of the wickedness and abominations of the people. Wherefore the book shall be kept from them.

"But the book shall be delivered unto a man, and he shall deliver the words of the book, which are the words of those who have slumbered in the dust, and he shall deliver these words unto another;

"But the words which are sealed he shall not deliver, neither shall he deliver the book. For the book shall be sealed by the power of God, and the revelation which was sealed shall be kept in the book until the own due time of the Lord, that they may come forth; for behold, they reveal all things from the foundation of the world unto the end thereof.

"And the day cometh that the words of the book which were sealed shall be read upon the house tops; and they shall be read by the power of Christ; and all things shall be revealed unto the children of men which ever have been among the children of men, and which ever will be even unto the end of the earth.

"Wherefore, at that day when the book shall be delivered unto the man of whom I have spoken, the book shall be hid from the eyes of the world, that the eyes of none shall behold it save it be that three witnesses shall behold it, by the power of God, besides him to whom the book shall be delivered; and they shall testify to the truth of the book and the things therein.

"And there is none other which shall view it, save it be a few according to the will of God, to bear testimony of his word unto the children of men; for the Lord God hath said that the words of the faithful should speak as if it were from the dead.

"Wherefore, the Lord God will proceed to bring forth the words of the book; and in the mouth of as many witnesses as seemeth him good will he establish his word; and wo be unto him that rejecteth the word of God!

"But behold, it shall come to pass that the Lord God shall say unto him to whom he shall deliver the book: Take these words which are not sealed and deliver them to another, that he may show them unto the learned, saying: Read this, I pray thee. And the learned shall say; Bring hither the book, and I will read them." (2 Nephi 27:5-15.)

Nephi explained, as is noted, that three witnesses would be chosen of the Lord to view this ancient record and as many others "as seemeth me good." Note now these additional words:

"And now, because of the glory of the world and to get gain will they say this, and not for the glory of God.

"And the man shall say: I cannot bring the book, for it is sealed.

"Then shall the learned say: I cannot read it.

"Wherefore it shall come to pass, that the Lord God will deliver again the book and the words thereof to him that is not learned; and the man that is not learned shall say: I am not learned.

"Then shall the Lord God say unto him: The learned shall not read them, for they have rejected them, and I am able to do mine own work; wherefore thou shalt read the words which I shall give unto thee.

"Touch not the things which are sealed, for I will bring them forth in mine own due time; for I will show unto the children of men that I am able to do mine own work." (2 Nephi 27:16-21.)

How easily understood are these words. Do they not remove all mystery from Isaiah's expressions? Are they not in plain language and in great detail? Of course the Book of Mormon is required to give clarity to Isaiah, and it does so amazingly well!

Now Nephi continues:

"Wherefore, when thou hast read the words which I have commanded thee, and obtained the witnesses which I have promised unto thee, then shalt thou seal up the book again, and hide it up unto me, that I may preserve the words which thou hast not read, until I shall see fit in mine own wisdom to reveal all things unto the children of men.

"For behold, I am God; and I am a God of miracles; and I will show unto the world that I am the same yesterday, today, and forever; and I work not among the children of men save it be according to their faith.

"And again it shall come to pass that the Lord shall

say unto him that shall read the words that shall be delivered him:

"Forasmuch as this people draw near unto me with their mouth, and with their lips do honor me, but have removed their hearts far from me, and their fear towards me is taught by the precepts of men—

"Therefore, I will proceed to do a marvelous work among this people, yea, a marvelous work and a wonder, for the wisdom of their wise and learned shall perish, and the understanding of their prudent shall be hid." (2 Nephi 27:22-26.)

Both Isaiah and Nephi point out that this sacred record which would come "out of the ground," and which would permit a nation once destroyed to speak suddenly in a modern voice, will actually appear shortly *before* Lebanon shall become a fruitful field. It is thus dated in prophecy.

Palestine "blossomed as the rose" only after the Jews began colonization there. That followed World War I and was brought about through the Balfour treaty between the United States and Great Britain in the 1920s. However, the Book of Mormon was printed in 1830, nearly a century before Palestine was freed from the Turks. In the Lord's language, that is but a "little while," as the prophet says.

It is interesting also that both Isaiah and Nephi explain that the deaf shall "hear the words of the book, and the eyes of the blind shall see out of obscurity and out of darkness." (2 Nephi 27:29; Isaiah 29:18.)

The blind, with Braille, now read the Book of Mormon, and modern hearing devices, including the sign language, allow the deaf to learn the message of the book. Of course, in the parabolic sense in which the scriptures so often speak, the passage may also mean that those who formerly were blind to the truth and those who formerly were deaf to the gospel, in that they refused to see or listen to it, would now see and hear and be convinced, this by the blessing of God.

And as both prophets so plainly taught, "the meek

also shall increase . . . their joy . . . in the Lord, and the poor among men shall rejoice in the Holy One of Israel." (2 Nephi 27:30; Isaiah 29:19.) This would be an important part of the "marvellous work and a wonder."

How were all these prophetic words fulfilled?

The account of the translation and publication of the Book of Mormon provides the evidence that the Book of Mormon was that ancient record. The Prophet Joseph Smith gives the details plainly in his *History of the Church*. Each facet set forth by Israel and Nephi is verified in the actual events that developed during the publication of the Book of Mormon.

Joseph Smith was the unlearned man.

Professor Charles Anthon of Columbia College was the learned man.

Martin Harris took only some of the words of the book to Professor Anthon.

Three witnesses were chosen to view the record, to which they gave their solemn testimony. As was indicated, there would also be other witnesses. Eight were chosen, and they handled and carefully scrutinized the ancient record and testified of its existence.

This is all a mighty fulfillment of prophecy in the words of both Isaiah and Nephi. The Bible thus bears testimony to the Book of Mormon. In this regard, Ezekiel joins Isaiah in describing this additional volume of scripture. (See Ezekiel 37:16-28.)

The Book of Mormon also bears testimony to the accuracy of the Bible. And both volumes fully sustain the account of the restoration of the gospel.

The Book of Mormon is verily true, brought forth literally by the power of God. All the details of its identification provided by Isaiah were fully met. That book *did* come out of the ground. It *does* speak for a people suddenly destroyed. It has a mighty message to all mankind.

That message is and forever shall be: Jesus Christ of Nazareth is the Son of God! He is our Savior, the Redeemer of all flesh!

Chapter Twenty-one

THE UNLEARNED MAN

By the time Joseph Smith closed his career in martyrdom, he was brilliant and he was learned. He had been taught by heavenly angels and by the Holy Spirit as well.

When the Saints settled in Kirtland, Ohio, one of their first efforts was to provide for education, and a school of the prophets was begun. Later, when they established the city of Nauvoo, Illinois, they organized the University of Nauvoo. The Prophet Joseph was a firm supporter of education and took every opportunity to study ancient languages and other subjects.

But when, as a youth, he was selected as the one through whom the Lord would usher into the world "a marvelous work and a wonder," he most certainly was unschooled and unlearned. Isaiah could not have described him more accurately.

To suppose that he had the capacity to *write* the Book of Mormon, or any book for that matter, was simply beyond reason, especially when it is remembered what archaeologists subsequently found in Book of Mormon lands, and when we discover that the book is filled with Hebrew idioms of which the young farm boy had not the slightest inkling. His formal classroom education would not exceed even the sixth grade as we know it.

The translation was nothing short of a miracle, and of course that is what the Lord called it. He did that work by the gift and power of God, and not of any man or set of men. (See D&C 3:11-14; 5:4; 6:25; 10:1-3.)

Joseph Smith was raised in a poor family, all members of which were obliged to work to bring home the required daily sustenance. Not only did he work on his

father's farm, but he also hired out as a laborer to his
neighbors.

The schools that were available at that time were
usually of the one-room variety, and even these Joseph
was not able to attend regularly.

During most of his childhood he lived in areas that
were, in fact, frontier regions of the struggling young
United States of America, where schools were scarce
and far between. Few of the young people in those areas
at that time attended school with any degree of regulari-
ty. Their conditions were not too different from those of
Abraham Lincoln.

It was to such a young man that the Lord entrusted
the publication of this ancient record that was destined to
come out of the ground and out of the dust, baffling even
the wise and prudent men of the world.

People who knew the Prophet Joseph Smith in his
childhood confirmed that he was not privileged to have
much schooling, and his own family, of course, knew
very well his childhood educational limitations, for his
brothers and sisters suffered the same handicap.

And when notoriety was given to his connection with
the "golden Bible," much was published in the newspapers about his being unlearned. Shortly after the appearance of the Book of Mormon, several other books
were published also that claimed to "expose" the fallacy
of Joseph's story.

These books and newspapers spared no effort to "reveal" that Joseph was an unlettered and unlearned farm
laborer, and that his claims to supernatural events were
false. The authors apparently took delight in trying to
prove the young man's complete inadequacy to produce
any book.

Whereas this resulted in persecution to Joseph and
his family, it nevertheless serves as evidence of the truth
of what Isaiah said. Of course Joseph was an unlearned
man, and now these newspapers and books proved it.

One of the books that allegedly exposed the Prophet

was *The Origin, Rise and Progress of Mormonism* by Pomeroy Tucker, published in Palmyra, New York.

Gleanings by the Way, written by the Reverend John A. Clark, a resident of Palmyra, freely quoted neighbors in the area concerning the character and economic burdens of the entire Smith family.

And what do such books prove? That Joseph was unlearned when he produced the Book of Mormon, just as Isaiah said. But they also prove that Joseph did indeed have a manuscript to be published as a book, although at first few people would take him seriously.

Ellen E. Dickinson wrote a book entitled *New Light on Mormonism* in which she quoted Thurlow Weed, famous New York politician and publisher, as follows: "In 1825 [later corrected to 1829] when I was publishing the Rochester *Telegraph* a man introduced himself to me as Joseph Smith, of Palmyra, N.Y., whose object, he said, was to get a book published. He then stated he had been guided by a vision to a spot he described, where, in a cavern, he found what he called a golden Bible." (New York: Funk and Wagnalls, 1885, p. 260.) Mr. Weed examined the manuscript and refused to publish it.

In 1834 a book entitled *Mormonism Unvailed* was written by Eber D. Howe, a printer of Painesville, Ohio, only nine miles from Kirtland, where the Saints were then living. He quoted in his book affidavits from Palmyra citizens attacking the character of Joseph Smith and asserting that he was "an ignorant person, a fraud and a deceiver." (See Francis W. Kirkham, *A New Witness for Christ in America,* 3rd ed., 1951, 1:130.)

Emphasizing that Joseph was unlearned, Tucker in his book went so far as to say: "Smith could not write in a legible hand, and hence an amanuensis or scribe was necessary. Cowdery had been a schoolmaster, and was the only man in the band who could make a copy for the printer." (Kirkham, 1:114.)

Defamatory articles were published in the Rochester *Advertiser and Telegraph* on August 31, 1829; in the

Palmyra *Freeman;* and in the Rochester *Gem* on September 5, 1829. And what do they prove?

Although they attack the young prophet, the publications are solid evidence that he had a manuscript, that he regarded it as miraculous, and that he himself was not an educated man, but rather a humble farmer without any previous publication experience.

Joseph's mother says in her own life story of the Prophet that he was not learned, and Joseph's wife agreed. She assisted at times with the translation when no other scribe was available.

Dr. Francis W. Kirkham, in his book *A New Witness for Christ in America,* quotes members of the family as well as close associates of the Prophet, setting forth facts concerning the translation of the Book of Mormon and the manner in which the work was accomplished. In all cases it is made clear that Joseph had *not* the capacity to produce the book on his own, but that it was done by the power of God. Dr. Kirkham writes as follows:

Regarding this fact Professor N. L. Nelson writes:

"Joseph Smith dictated the Book of Mormon without apparent hesitation, as fast as a scribe could write it in long hand. There is no chance of error on this point. The entire Whitmer family, besides Olivery Cowdery, Martin Harris, and Joseph's wife, sat and listened, or had free access to listen, to the record as it grew day by day during the entire month of June, 1829." (N. L. Nelson, *Mormon Point of View,* p. 124.)

A direct statement confirming this fact has been left us by Emma Smith Bidamon, the wife of the Prophet Joseph Smith. The questions to her were by her son, Joseph Smith, and were asked in the presence of Bishop Rogers, W. W. Blair, and H. A. Stebbins. A part of the interview follows:

"Q. Could not Father have dictated the Book of Mormon to you, Oliver Cowdery, and others who wrote for him after having first written it, or having first read it out of some book?

"A. Joseph Smith could neither write nor dictate a coherent and well worded letter, let alone dictating a book like the Book of Mormon, and though I was an active participant in the scenes that transpired, and was present during the translating of the plates, and had cognizance of things as they transpired, it is marvelous to me, "a marvel and a wonder," as much so as to anyone else. (A private

journal written by Joseph Smith in his own hand writing is evidence
of the above statement. This journal is preserved in the Historian's
Office, Salt Lake City, Utah.)

"Q. Mother, what is your belief about the authenticity, or origin of the Book of Mormon?

"A. My belief is that the Book of Mormon is of divine
authenticity—I have not the slightest doubt of it. I am satisfied that
no man could have dictated the writing of the manuscript unless he
was inspired: for, when [I was acting] as his scribe, your father
would dictate to me hour after hour; and when returning after meals,
or after interruptions, he would at once begin where he had left off,
without either seeing the manuscript or having any portion of it
read to him. It would have been improbable that a learned man could
do this; and, for one so . . . unlearned as he was, it was simply
impossible.

"These questions and answers she had given to them, were read
to my mother by me, the day before my leaving Nauvoo for home
and were affirmed by her. Major Bidamon stated that he had frequently conversed with her on the subject of the translation of the
Book of Mormon, and her present answers were substantially what
she had always stated in regard to it.

Signed, JOSEPH SMITH, Who is the Son of the
Prophet Joseph Smith. (The Saints Advocate, Oct.,
1879)"

(Kirkham, *op. cit.*, pp. 194–96.)

Chapter Twenty-two

"ONE THAT IS LEARNED"

Martin Harris was greatly impressed by the Prophet Joseph Smith and the existence of the gold plates of the Book of Mormon. He assisted Joseph for a time as a scribe, and became especially curious as to the authenticity of the work.

He obtained from the Prophet the first 116 pages of the translated manuscript and showed them to his wife. The pages were lost, bringing the condemnation of the Lord upon both Martin and the young Prophet. As Martin was repentant, the Lord forgave him but did not permit him to serve further as scribe.

Martin felt that he should assist in financing the publication of the book, and he was willing to mortgage his farm to do so. But he wanted to have some further assurance that the work was all that Joseph claimed for it. He obtained from the Prophet a transcription of some of the characters as they appeared on the plates. These he intended to take to New York City, to submit to scholars, and thus satisfy himself as to their value. This he set out to do.

He obtained from the Prophet a transcript of some of the characters on the plates and took them to New York, where he showed them to two experts in ancient writings: Dr. Charles Anthon of Columbia College, now Columbia University, and Dr. Samuel L. Mitchell.

On his return, Martin made the following report:

I went to the city of New York and presented the characters which had been translated, with the translation thereof, to Professor Charles Anthon, a gentleman celebrated for his literary attainments. Professor Anthon stated that the translation was correct, more so than any he had before seen translated from the Egyptian. I then showed him those which were not yet translated and he said that they were Egyptian, Chaldaic, Assyrian and Arabic; and he stated they were true characters.

He gave me a certificate, certifying to the people of Palmyra that they were true characters, and that the translation of such of them as had been translated was also correct. I took the certificate and put it into my pocket, and was just leaving the house, when Mr. Anthon called me back, and asked me how the young man found out that there were gold places in the place where he found them. I answered that an angel of God had revealed it unto him.

He then said to me, "Let me see that certificate." I accordingly took it out of my pocket and gave it to him, when he took it and tore it to pieces, saying that there was no such thing now as ministering of angels, and that if I would bring the plates to him, he would translate them. I informed him that part of the plates were sealed, and that I was forbidden to bring them. He replied, "I cannot read a sealed book."

I left him and went to Mr. Mitchell, who sanctioned what Professor Anthon had said, respecting both the characters and the translation. (Joseph Fielding Smith, *Essentials in Church History,* Deseret Book, 1974, p. 54.)

Evidently the Saints quoted Martin Harris concerning his New York visit, and eventually word reached Professor Anthon to this effect. He resented it and denied what Martin had said, although he did admit a recollection of the visit. Years later he wrote a letter setting forth his denial and providing other details concerning the episode.

One of the very interesting things he wrote in his letter is that the characters copied by Joseph Smith and delivered to Martin Harris were in vertical columns, not horizontal. This is of vital importance in view of the recent discovery, in an old Bible, of what is regarded as the original paper that Harris took to Anthon. This paper shows the characters to be in *vertical columns* also. Although this statement has been in Anthon's letter, resting in the Church archives for decades, no interest was shown in the fact that the characters were in vertical columns until the original was found in an old Bible by Mark William Hofmann, who had bought it as a curiosity, not knowing that it contained the document.

The letter was written to Anthon's friend the Reverend Dr. Coit, rector of Trinity Church, New Rochelle, New York. This letter was first published by the Reverend J. A. Clark in his book *Gleanings by the Way,* and has been reprinted in Francis W. Kirkham's *A New Witness for Christ in America* (1:417-21). Dated New York, April 3, 1841, it reads as follows:

Rev. and Dear Sir:

I have often heard that the Mormons claimed me for an auxiliary, but, as no one, until the present time, has ever requested from me a statement in writing, I have not deemed it worth while to say anything publicly on the subject. What I do know of the sect relates to some of their early movements; and as the facts may amuse you, while they will furnish a satisfactory answer to the charge of my being a Mormon proselyte, I proceed to lay them before you in detail.

Many years ago, the precise date I do not now recollect, a plain looking countryman called upon me with a letter from Dr. Samuel L. Mitchell requesting me to examine, and give my opinion upon, a certain paper, marked with various characters which the Doctor confessed he could not decipher, and which the bearer of the note was very anxious to have explained. A very brief examination of the paper convinced me that it was a mere hoax, and a very clumsy one too.

The characters *were arranged in columns, like the Chinese mode of writing, and presented the most singular medley that I ever beheld.* Greek, Hebrew, and all sorts of letters, more or less distorted, either through unskilfulness, or from actual design, were intermingled with sundry delineations of half moons, stars, and other natural objects, and the whole ended in a rude representation of the Mexican zodiac.

The conclusion was irresistible, that some cunning fellow had prepared the paper in question, for the purpose of imposing upon the countryman who brought it, and I told the man so without any hesitation. He then proceeded to give me a history of the whole affair, which convinced me that he had fallen into the hands of some sharper, while it left me in great astonishment at his own simplicity.

The countryman told me that a gold book had been recently dug up in the western or northern part (I forget which), of our state, and he described this book as consisting of many gold plates, like leaves, secured by a gold wire passing through the edge of each, just as the leaves of a book are sewed together, and presented in this way the appearance of a volume. Each plate, according to him, was inscribed with unknown characters, and the paper which he handed me, a transcript of one of these pages.

On my asking him by whom the copy was made, he gravely stated, that along with the golden book there had been dug up a very large pair of spectacles! so large in fact that if a man were to hold them in front of his face, his two eyes would merely look through one of the glasses, and the remaining part of the spectacles would project a considerable distance sideways! These spectacles possessed, it seems a very valuable property, of enabling any one who looked through them, (or rather through one of the lenses), not only to decipher the characters on the plates, but also to comprehend their exact meaning, and be able to translate them!

My informant assured me that this curious property of the spectacles had been actually tested, and found to be true. A young man, it seems, had been placed in the garret of a farm house, with a curtain before him, and having fastened the spectacles to his head, had read several pages in the golden book, and communicated their contents in writing to certain persons stationed on the outside of the curtain.

He had also copied off one page of the book in the original character, which he had in like manner handed over to those who were separated from him by the curtain, and this copy was the paper which the countryman had brought with him. As the golden book was said to contain very great truths, and most important revelations of a religious nature, a strong desire had been expressed by several persons in the countryman's neighborhood, to have the whole work translated and published. A proposition had accordingly been made to my informant, to sell his farm, and apply the proceeds to the printing of the golden book, and the golden plates were to be left with him as security until he should be reimbursed by the sale of the work.

To convince him more clearly that there was no risk whatever in the matter, and that the work was actually what it claimed to be, he was told to take the paper, which purported to be a copy of the pages of the book, to the city of New York, and submit it to the learned in that quarter, who would soon dispel all his doubts, and satisfy him as to the perfect safety of the investment.

As Dr. Mitchell was our "Magnus Apollo" in those days, the man called first upon him; but the Doctor, evidently suspecting some trick, declined giving any opinion about the matter, and sent the countryman down to the college, to see, in all probability, what the "learned pundits" in that place would make of the affair.

On my telling the bearer of the paper that an attempt had been made to impose on him, and defraud him of his property, he requested me to give him my opinion in writing about the paper which he had shown to me. I did so without any hesitation, partly for the man's sake, and partly to let the individual "behind the curtain," see that his trick was discovered.

The import of what I wrote was, as far as I can now recollect, simply this, that the marks in the paper appeared to be merely an imitation of various alphabetical characters, and had, in my opinion, no meaning at all connected with them. The countryman then took his leave, with many thanks, and with the express declaration that he would in no shape part with his farm or embark in the speculation of printing the golden book.

The matter rested here for a considerable time, until one day, when I had ceased entirely to think of the countryman and his paper, this same individual, to my great surprise, paid me a second visit. He now brought with him a duodecimo volume, which he said was a translation into English of the "Golden Bible." He also stated, that notwithstanding his original determination not to sell his farm, he had been induced eventually to do so, and apply the money to the publication of the book, and had received the golden plates as a security for repayment.

He begged my acceptance of the volume, assuring me that it would be found extremely interesting, and that it was already "making a great noise" in the upper part of the state. Suspecting now that some serious trick was on foot, and that my plain-looking visitor might be in fact a very cunning fellow I declined his present and merely contented myself with a slight examination of the volume while he stood by.

The more I declined receiving it however, the more urgent the man became in offering the book, until at last I told him plainly, that if he left the volume, as he said he intended to do, I should most assuredly throw it after him as he departed. I then asked him how he could be so foolish as to sell his farm and engage in this affair; and requested him to tell me if the plates were really gold.

In answer to this latter inquiry, he said that he had never seen the plates themselves, which were carefully locked up in a trunk, but that he had the trunk in his possession. I advised him by all means to open the trunk and examine the contents, and if the plates proved to be of gold, which I did not believe at all, to sell them immediately.

His reply was, that if he opened the trunk the "curse of heaven would descend upon him and his children." "However," added he, "I will agree to open it, provided you will take the 'curse of heaven' upon yourself for having advised me to the step." I told him I was perfectly willing to do so, and begged he would hasten home and examine the trunk, for he would find he had been cheated. He promised to do as I recommended, and left me, taking his book with him. I have never seen him since.

Such is a plain statement of all that I know respecting the Mormons. My impression now is, that the plain looking countryman was none other than the prophet Smith himself, who assumed an appearance of great simplicity in order to entrap me, if possible, into some recommendation of his book. That the prophet aided me by his inspiration, in interpreting the volume, is only one of the many amusing falsehoods which the Mormonites utter relative to my participation in their doctrines. Of these doctrines I know nothing whatever, nor have I ever heard a single discourse from any one of their preachers, although I have often felt a strong curiosity to become an auditor, since my friends tell me that they frequently name me in their sermons, and even go so far as to say that I am alluded to in the prophecies of Scripture!

If what I have here written shall prove of any service in opening the eyes of some of their deluded followers to the real designs of those who profess to be the apostles of Mormonism, it will afford me a satisfaction, equalled, I have no doubt only by that which you yourself will feel on this subject.

I remain very respectfully and truly, your friend,
Chas. Anthon.

It is obvious that the letter is full of errors and false claims, evidently to save face for Professor Anthon. But the fact is clearly affirmed that Martin Harris did visit him and did show him the transcripts, that the "gold book" came out of the ground, and that the transcriptions were in vertical columns, a point of great interest.

When Professor Anthon said he could not read a sealed book, Isaiah was vindicated and so was the Book of Mormon in the light of the biblical prophecy. The story of the "learned man," as well as that of the "unlearned man," is vital to a proper identification of the Book of Mormon, testifying that the volume is all that is claimed for it.

It was King David of old who said, "Truth shall spring out of the earth; and righteousness shall look down from heaven." (Psalm 85:11.)

ONLY BY
DIVINE POWER

The Lord himself affirms that it was only by the power of God that Joseph Smith was able to translate the ancient record.

The volume was written in a tongue unknown to modern men, in what those ancients themselves called Reformed Egyptian, and was not known to any other people. Not even the scholars of Joseph's day could decipher the inscriptions that had been copied off by him and shown to others by Martin Harris. Only by the power of God could they be translated.

This is made clear by the Lord. In Doctrine and Covenants 1:29, we read: "And after having received the record of the Nephites, yea, even my servant Joseph Smith, Jun., might have power to translate through the mercy of God, by the power of God, the Book of Mormon."

In section 9 we have the following, referring to Oliver Cowdery:

"But, behold, I say unto you, that you must study it out in your mind; then you must ask me if it be right, and if it is right I will cause that your bosom shall burn within you; therefore, you shall feel that it is right.

"But if it be not right you shall have no such feelings, but you shall have a stupor of thought that shall cause you to forget the thing which is wrong; therefore, you cannot write that which is sacred save it be given you from me.

"Now, if you had known this you could have translated; nevertheless, it is not expedient that you should translate now. Behold, it was expedient when you commenced; but you feared, and the time is past, and it is not expedient now; for, do you not behold that I have given unto my servant Joseph sufficient strength, whereby it is made up? And neither of you have I condemned.'' (Verses 8-12.)

Although these words are addressed to Oliver Cowdery, they reinforce the principle that translation of sacred things cannot be accomplished except ''it be given you from me.''

When Martin Harris's wife lost the first 116 pages of translated manuscript, the Lord upbraided Joseph severely. First he made it clear that Joseph's ability to translate was strictly a gift of God: ''Now, behold, I say unto you, that because you delivered up those writings which you had power given unto you to translate by the means of the Urim and Thummim, into the hands of a wicked man, you have lost them.'' (D&C 10:1.)

Then the Lord took that gift from the Prophet so that he became powerless to translate further until commanded to do so: ''And you also lost your gift at the same time, and your mind became darkened. Nevertheless, it is now restored unto you again; therefore see that you are faithful and continue on unto the finishing of the remainder of the work of translation as you have begun. Do not run faster or labor more than you have strength and means provided to enable you to translate; but be diligent unto the end.'' (D&C 10:2-4. See also D&C 3:11 14, 5:4, 6:25.) It was indeed a gift.

The Lord gave detailed instructions on how to proceed:

''Behold, I say unto you, that you shall not translate again those words which have gone forth out of your hands; . . .

''Therefore, you shall translate the engravings which are on the plates of Nephi, down even till you come to the reign of king Benjamin, or until you come to that which you have translated, which you have retained; and behold, you shall publish it as the record of Nephi; and thus I will confound those who have altered my words. . . .

"Behold, there are many things engraven upon the plates of Nephi which do throw greater views upon my gospel; therefore, it is wisdom in me that you should translate this first part of the engravings of Nephi, and send forth in this work." (D&C 10:30, 41-42, 45.)

The fact that the power to translate was strictly a gift to Joseph Smith is further stated by the Lord in these words:

"Behold, thou art Joseph, and thou wast chosen to do the work of the Lord, but because of transgression, if thou art not aware thou wilt fall.

"But remember, God is merciful; therefore, repent of that which thou hast done which is contrary to the commandment which I gave you, and thou art still chosen, and art again called to the work; except thou do this, thou shalt be delivered up and become as other men, and have no more gift.

"And when thou deliveredst up that which God had given thee sight and power to translate, thou deliveredst up that which was sacred into the hands of a wicked man." (D&C 3:9-12.)

This, of course, was said in regard to the loss of the 116 pages of manuscript. But it illustrates the fact that Joseph translated only by the gift of God through the Urim and Thummim.

At other times the Lord spoke about the fact that it was *he,* God, who had brought forth the Book of Mormon. As he spoke to the witnesses of the Book of Mormon he said:

"And ye shall testify that you have seen them, even as my servant Joseph Smith, Jun., has seen them; for it is by my power that he has seen them, and it is because he had faith.

"And he has translated the book, even that part which I have commanded him, and as your Lord and your God liveth it is true.

"Wherefore, you have received the same power, and the same faith, and the same gift like unto him;

"And if you do these last commandments of mine, which I have given you, the gates of hell shall not prevail against you; for my grace is sufficient for you, and you shall be lifted up at the last day.

"And I, Jesus Christ, your Lord and your God, have spoken it unto you, that I might bring about my righteous purposes unto the children of men. Amen." (D&C 17:5-9.)

Again, when the Lord gave commandments to Martin Harris concerning the financing of the printing of the Book of Mormon, he spoke as follows, again declaring that the book contains his word, which, of course, was brought about only by his power:

"And again, I commanded thee that thou shalt not covet thine own property, but impart it freely to the printing of the Book of Mormon, which contains the truth and the word of God—

"Which is my word to the Gentile, that soon it may go to the Jew, of whom the Lamanites are a remnant, that they may believe the gospel, and look not for a Messiah to come who has already come." (D&C 19:26-27.)

To say that the young Joseph Smith produced the Book of Mormon through his own efforts is to completely ignore the facts. It was an act of God, a "marvelous work and a wonder."

Chapter Twenty-four

DESTROYED SUDDENLY

The Book of Mormon tells of the branch of the House of Israel that God brought from Palestine to America about six hundred years before Christ. The prophet Lehi was their leader.

The family grew to be a great nation. Divisions developed, however, and the nation broke in two. One faction was known as the Nephites, usually the more righteous. The other was called Lamanites, after their original wicked leader.

Over the years the Nephites and the Lamanites battled each other. Prophets came among both groups; some were killed, while most were ignored, although there were periods of righteousness.

The Savior appeared to the Nephites after his resurrection in Palestine. This miraculous event brought universal peace in the land as both factions were converted to Christ. This peace lasted for two hundred years, when again divisions arose, wickedness increased, and wars were resumed.

The Nephites became the more wicked of the two. The Lord warned them that if they did not repent, he would permit the Lamanites to destroy them all in battle—men, women, and children. They did not heed the prophets, but continued with their wars and wickedness.

The final story of their destruction in battle is told by Mormon, the prophet who compiled the Book of Mormon, and who at the time was the commanding general of the Nephites. He wrote as follows:

"And now I finish my record concerning the destruction of my people, the Nephites. And it came to pass that we did march forth before the Lamanites.

"And I, Mormon, wrote an epistle unto the king of the Lamanites, and desired of him that he would grant unto us that we might gather together our people unto the land of Cumorah, by a hill which was called Cumorah, and there we could give them battle.

"And it came to pass that the king of the Lamanites did grant unto me the thing which I desired.

"And it came to pass that we did march forth to the land of Cumorah, and we did pitch our tents around about the hill Cumorah; and it was in a land of many waters, rivers, and fountains; and here we had hope to gain advantage over the Lamanites.

"And when three hundred and eighty and four years had passed away, we had gathered in all the remainder of our people unto the land of Cumorah.

"And it came to pass that when we had gathered in all our people in one to the land of Cumorah, behold I, Mormon, began to be old; and knowing it to be the last struggle of my people, and having been commanded of the Lord that I should not suffer the records which had been handed down by our fathers, which were sacred, to fall into the hands of the Lamanites, (for the Lamanites would destroy them) therefore I made this record out of the plates of Nephi, and hid up in the hill Cumorah all the records which had been entrusted to me by the hand of the Lord, save it were these few plates which I gave unto my son Moroni.

"And it came to pass that my people, with their wives and their children, did now behold the armies of the Lamanites marching towards them; and with that awful fear of death which fills the breasts of all the wicked, did they await to receive them.

"And it came to pass that they came to battle against us, and every soul was filled with terror because of the greatness of their numbers.

"And it came to pass that they did fall upon my

people with the sword, and with the bow, and with the arrow, and with the ax, and with all manner of weapons of war.

"And it came to pass that my men were hewn down, yea, even my ten thousand who were with me, and I fell wounded in the midst; and they passed by me that they did not put an end to my life.

"And when they had gone through and hewn down all my people save it were twenty and four of us, (among whom was my son Moroni) and we having survived the dead of our people, did behold on the morrow, when the Lamanites had returned unto their camps, from the top of the hill Cumorah, the ten thousand of my people who were hewn down, being led in the front by me.

"And we also beheld the ten thousand of my people who were led by my son Moroni.

"And behold, the ten thousand of Gidgiddonah had fallen, and he also in the midst.

"And Lamah had fallen with his ten thousand; and Gilgal had fallen with his ten thousand; and Limhah had fallen with his ten thousand; and Joneam had fallen with his ten thousand; and Camenihah, and Moronihah, and Antionum, and Shiblom, and Shem, and Josh, had fallen with their ten thousand each.

"And it came to pass that there were ten more who did fall by the sword, with their ten thousand each; yea, even all my people, save it were those twenty and four who were with me, and also a few who had escaped into the south countries, and a few who had deserted over unto the Lamanites, had fallen; and their flesh, and bones, and blood lay upon the face of the earth, being left by the hands of those who slew them to molder upon the land, and to crumble and to return to their mother earth.

"And my soul was rent with anguish, because of the slain of my people, and I cried:

"O ye fair ones, how could ye have departed from the ways of the Lord! O ye fair ones, how could ye have rejected that Jesus, who stood with open arms to receive you!

"Behold, if ye had not done this, ye would not have fallen. But behold, ye are fallen, and I mourn your loss.

"O ye fair sons and daughters, ye fathers and mothers, ye husbands and wives, ye fair ones, how is it that ye could have fallen!

"But behold, ye are gone, and my sorrows cannot bring your return.

"And the day soon cometh that your mortal must put on immortality, and these bodies which are now moldering in corruption must soon become incorruptible bodies; and then ye must stand before the judgment-seat of Christ to be judged according to your works; and if it so be that ye are righteous, then are ye blessed with your fathers who have gone before you

"O that ye had repented before this great destruction had come upon you. But behold, ye are gone, and the Father, yea, he Eternal Father of heaven, knoweth your state; and he doeth with you according to his justice and mercy." (Mormon 6.)

Moroni, son of Mormon, was the sole survivor of the conflict. It was he who concluded the writings on the gold plates and then buried them in the ground for safekeeping. He wrote as follows:

"Behold I, Moroni, do finish the record of my father, Mormon. Behold, I have but few things to write, which things I have been commanded by my father.

"And now it came to pass that after the great and tremendous battle at Cumorah, behold, the Nephites who had escaped into the country southward were hunted by the Lamanites, until they were all destroyed.

"And my father also was killed by them, and I even remain alone to write the sad tale of the destruction of my people. But behold, they are gone, and I fulfil the commandment of my father. And whether they will slay me, I know not.

"Therefore I will write and hide up the records in the earth; and whither I go it mattereth not.

"Behold, my father hath made this record, and he hath written the intent thereof. And behold, I would write it also if I had room upon the plates, but I have not; and ore I have none, for I am alone. My father hath been slain in battle, and all my kinsfolk, and I have not friends nor whither to go; and how long the Lord will suffer that I may live I know not.

"Behold, four hundred sears have passed away since the coming of our Lord and Savior.

"And behold, the Lamanites have hunted my people, the Nephites, down from city to city and from place to place, even until they are no more; and great has been their fall; yea, great and marvelous is the destruction of my people, the Nephites.

"And behold, it is the hand of the Lord which hath done it. And behold also, the Lamanites are at war one with another; and the whole face of this land is one continual round of murder and bloodshed; and no one knoweth the end of the war.

"And now, behold, I say no more concerning them, for there are none save it be the Lamanites and robbers that do exist upon the face of the land.

"And there are none that do know the true God save it be the disciples of Jesus, who did tarry in the land until the wickedness of the people was so great that the Lord would not suffer them to remain with the people; and whether they be upon the face of the land no man knoweth.

"But behold, my father and I have seen them, and they have ministered unto us.

"And whoso receiveth this record, and shall not condemn it because of the imperfections which are in it, the same shall know of greater things than these. Behold, I am Moroni; and were it possible, I would make all things known unto you.

"Behold, I make an end of speaking concerning this people. I am the son of Mormon, and my father was a descendant of Nephi.

"And I am the same who hideth up this record unto the Lord; the plates thereof are of no worth, because of the commandment of the Lord. For he truly saith that no one shall have them to get gain; but the record thereof is of great worth; and whoso shall bring it to light, him will the Lord bless.

"For none can have power to bring it to light save it be given him of God; for God wills that it shall be done with an eye single to his glory, or the welfare of the ancient and long dispersed covenant people of the Lord.

"And blessed be he that shall bring this thing to light; for it shall be brought out of darkness unto light, according to the word of God; yea, it shall be brought out of the earth, and it shall shine forth out of darkness, and come unto the knowledge of the people; and it shall be done by the power of God.

"And if there be faults they be the faults of a man. But behold, we know no fault; nevertheless God knoweth all things; therefore, he that condemneth, let him be aware lest he shall be in danger of hell fire." (Mormon 8:1-17.)

It is not known how long Moroni wandered alone in the earth following the destruction of his nation, but as he closed up the record before his passing he wrote:

"And I seal up these records, after I have spoken a few words by way of exhortation unto you.

"Behold, I would exhort you that when ye shall read these things, if it be wisdom in God that ye should read them, that ye would remember how merciful the Lord hath been unto the children of men, from the creation of Adam even down unto the time that ye shall receive these things, and ponder it in your hearts.

"And when ye shall receive these things, I would exhort you that ye would ask God, the Eternal Father, in the name of Christ, if these things are not true; and if ye shall ask with a sincere heart, with real intent, having faith in Christ, he will manifest the truth of it unto you, by the power of the Holy Ghost.

"And by the power of the Holy Ghost ye may know the truth of all things. . . .

"And now I bid unto all, farewell. I soon go to rest in the paradise of God, until my spirit and body shall again reunite, and I am brought forth triumphant through the air, to meet you before the pleasing bar of the great Jehovah, the Eternal Judge of both quick and dead. Amen." (Moroni 10:2-5, 34.)

Isaiah's words were fulfilled to the letter. The people who wrote the Book of Mormon were indeed destroyed "at an instant suddenly." (Isaiah 29:5.) The book was sealed and placed in the ground for safekeeping by the last survivor of the Nephite nation—Moroni.

Chapter Twenty-five

"WE HAVE GOT A BIBLE..."

By the inspiration of heaven, Nephi enlarged on the theme presented in chapter 29 of Isaiah. Again he spoke of the book that should come from the earth and serve as a modern voice for an ancient people who had been destroyed suddenly.

"The things which shall be written out of the book," Nephi declared, "shall be of great worth unto the children of men, and especially unto our seed, which is a remnant of the house of Israel." (2 Nephi 28:2.)

Speaking of the day in which the book would appear he said:

"For it shall come to pass in that day that the churches which are built up, and not unto the Lord, when the one shall say unto the other: Behold, I, I am the Lord's; and the others shall say: I, I am the Lord's; and thus shall every one say that hath built up churches, and not unto the Lord—

"And they shall contend one with another; and their priests shall contend one with another, and they shall teach with their learning, and deny the Holy Ghost, which giveth utterance.

"And they deny the power of God, the Holy One of Israel; and they say unto the people: Hearken unto us, and hear ye our precept; for behold there is no God today, for the Lord and the Redeemer hath done his work, and he hath given his power unto men;

"Behold, hearken ye unto my precept; if they shall say there is a miracle wrought by the hand of the Lord, believe it not; for this day he is not a God of miracles; he hath done his work.

"Yea, and there shall be many which shall say: Eat, drink, and be merry, for tomorrow we die; and it shall be well with us.

"And there shall also be many which shall say: Eat, drink, and be merry; nevertheless, fear God—he will justify in committing a little sin; yea, lie a little, take advantage of one because of his words, dig a pit for thy neighbor; there is no harm in this; and do all these things, for tomorrow we die; and if it so be that we are guilty, God will beat us with a few stripes, and at last we shall be saved in the kingdom of God.

"Yea, and there shall be many which shall teach after this manner, false and vain and foolish doctrines, and shall be puffed up in their hearts, and shall seek deep to hide their counsels from the Lord; and their works shall be in the dark." (Verses 3-9.)

He spoke then of the judgments that will come to the world following that day:

"But behold, if the inhabitants of the earth shall repent of their wickedness and abominations they shall not be destroyed, saith the Lord of Hosts.

"But behold, that great and abominable church, the whore of all the earth, must tumble to the earth, and great must be the fall thereof.

"For the kingdom of the devil must shake, and they which belong to it must needs be stirred up unto repentance, or the devil will grasp them with his everlasting chains, and they be stirred up to anger, and perish;

"For behold, at that day shall he rage in the hearts of the children of men, and stir them up to anger against that which is good.

"And others will he pacify, and lull them away into carnal security, that they will say: All is well in Zion; yea, Zion prospereth, all is well—and thus the devil cheateth their souls, and leadeth them away carefully down to hell.

"And behold, others he flattereth away, and telleth them there is no hell; and he saith unto them: I am no devil, for there is none—and thus he whispereth in their ears, until he grasps them with his awful chains, from whence there is no deliverance." (Verses 17-22.)

Coming back to a discussion of the book that is to be revealed, and the refusal of many to accept it, he says:

"Wo be unto him that shall say: We have received the word of God, and we need no more of the word of God, for we have enough!

"For behold, thus saith the Lord God: I will give unto the children of men line upon line, precept upon precept, here a little and there a little; and blessed are those who hearken unto my precepts, and lend an ear unto my counsel, for they shall learn wisdom; for unto him that receiveth I will give more; and from them that shall say, We have enough, from them shall be taken away even that which they have." (Verses 29-30.)

And then he says:

"But behold, there shall be many—at that day when I shall proceed to do a marvelous work among them, that I may remember my covenants which I have made unto the children of men, that I may set my hand again the second time to recover my people, which are of the house of Israel;

"And also, that I may remember the promises which I have made unto thee, Nephi, and also unto thy father, that I would remember your seed; and that the words of your seed should proceed forth out of my mouth unto your seed; and my words shall hiss forth unto the ends of the earth, for a standard unto my people, which are of the house of Israel;

"And because my words shall hiss forth—many of the Gentiles shall say: A Bible! A Bible! We have got a Bible, and there cannot be any more Bible.

"But thus saith the Lord God: O fools, they shall have a Bible; and it shall proceed forth from the Jews, mine ancient covenant people. And what thank they the Jews for the Bible which they receive from them? Yea, what do the Gentiles mean? Do they remember the travels, and the labors, and the pains of the Jews, and their diligence unto me, in bringing forth salvation unto the Gentiles? . . .

"Thou fool, that shall say: A Bible, we have got a Bible, and we need no more Bible. Have ye obtained a Bible save it were by the Jews?

"Know ye not that there are more nations than one? Know ye not that I, the Lord your God, have created all men, and that I remember those who are upon the isles of the sea; and that I rule in the heavens above and in the earth beneath; and I bring forth my word unto the children of men, yea, even upon all the nations of the earth?

"Wherefore murmur ye, because that ye shall receive more of my word? Know ye not that the testimony of two nations is a witness unto you that I am God, that I remember one nation like unto another? Wherefore, I speak the same words unto one nation like unto another. And when the two nations shall run together the testimony of the two nations shall run together also.

"And I do this that I may prove unto many that I am the same yesterday, today, and forever; and that I speak forth my words according to mine own pleasure. And because that I have spoken one word ye need not suppose that I cannot speak another; for my work is not yet finished; neither shall it be until the end of man, neither from that time henceforth and forever.

"Wherefore, because that ye have a Bible ye need not suppose that it contains all my words; neither need ye suppose that I have not caused more to be written.

"For I command all men, both in the east and in the west, and in the north, and in the south, and in the islands of the sea, that they shall write the words which I speak unto them; for out of the books which shall be written I will judge the world, every man according to their works, according to that which is written.

"For behold, I shall speak unto the Jews and they shall write it; and I shall also speak unto the Nephites and they shall write it; and I shall also speak unto the other tribes of the house of Israel, which I have led away, and they shall write it; and I shall also speak unto all nations of the earth and they shall write it.

"And it shall come to pass that the Jews shall have the words of the Nephites, and the Nephites shall have the words of the Jews; and the Nephites and the Jews shall have the words of the lost tribes of Israel; and the lost tribes of Israel shall have the words of the Nephites and the Jews.

"And it shall come to pass that my people which are of the house of Israel, shall be gathered home unto the lands of their possessions; and my word also shall be gathered in one. And I will show unto them that fight against my word and against my people, who are of the house of Israel, that I am God, and that I covenanted with Abraham that I would remember his seed forever." (2 Nephi 29:1-4, 6-14.)

Chapter Twenty-six

EZEKIEL'S STICKS

One of the greatest of God's purposes in the latter days is to gather the twelve tribes of Israel.

Many are the prophecies throughout the scriptures declaring that the Lord will bring about this mighty movement. The tribes are to gather to Palestine. Joseph will remain in America. Old Jerusalem will become a world capital in the Millennium. So also will the New Jerusalem, which is to be built at Jackson County, Missouri. The Savior is to govern from both.

Universal peace is predicted. The Savior, the Lord of all, will reign over a united Israel. There will be unity, with one fold and one Shepherd, and Jesus is that Shepherd.

As he gathers his people together in the last days, so their writings also are to be consolidated, bringing together the scriptures of the Jews, the Nephites, and the Lost Tribes. Each nation may read the writings of the other, with a common understanding. When this combining of all the scriptures is to be accomplished has not been revealed. (2 Nephi 29:13.)

One great first step in this direction was destined to *precede* the gathering of Israel and assist in bringing it about. Through it would come the testimony of the Savior, one nation to another, helping to establish Zion in the latter days in preparation for the second coming of Christ and the gathering of Israel.

This great first step is described by Isaiah and Ezekiel, and it relates to a volume of scripture known as the record of Joseph. The 29th chapter of Isaiah told the manner of its coming forth. Ezekiel identifies it and indicates that the volume will be an integral part of and preceding the final gathering.

As Ezekiel spoke of the gathering of the tribes, he wrote particularly of the Jews and the descendants of Joseph, Ephraim and Manasseh. Before the tribes come together, their records will be joined, eventually to become one in the hand of the Lord's servants. So Ezekiel spoke as follows:

"The word of the Lord came again unto me, saying, Moreover, thou son of man, take thee one stick, and write upon it, For Judah, and for the children of Israel his companions: then take another stick, and write upon it, For Joseph, the stick of Ephraim, and for all the house of Israel his companions: And join them one to another into one stick; and they shall become one in thine hand.

"And when the children of thy people shall speak unto thee, saying, Wilt thou not shew us what thou meanest by these?

"Say unto them, Thus saith the Lord God; Behold, I will take the stick of Joseph, which is in the hand of Ephraim, and the tribes of Israel his fellows, and will put them with him, even with the stick of Judah, and make them one stick, and they shall be one in mine hand." (Ezekiel 37:15-19.)

"Stick" seems to refer to both the people and their records.

Two kinds of "sticks" were associated with ancient writings among the house of Israel. One was that they actually wrote upon a piece of wood. Such "writing tablets" were in common use even in Babylon during the ministry of Ezekiel. The stick of Judah, then, would identify Judah as such, and yet it was itself a record.

The other was the type of stick about which parchment records were wound, as a scroll. This, too, was in common use among the house of Israel. It is believed that such a record or scroll was used by the Savior when he read from the prophets as he taught in the Jewish synagogues. (Luke 4:18.)

What is the record of the stick of Judah?

Nephi saw it in vision and was well acquainted with it. In the vision in First Nephi he wrote:

"I beheld a book, and it was carried forth among them.

"And the angel said unto me: Knowest thou the meaning of the book?

"And I said unto him: I know not.

"And he said: Behold it proceedeth out of the mouth of a Jew. And I, Nephi, beheld it; and he said unto me: The book that thou beholdest is a record of the Jews, which contains the covenants of the Lord, which he hath made unto the house of Israel; and it also containeth many of the prophecies of the holy prophets; and it is a record like unto the engravings which are upon the plates of brass, save there are not so many; nevertheless, they contain the covenants of the Lord, which he hath made unto the house of Israel; wherefore, they are of great worth unto the Gentiles.

"And the angel of the Lord said unto me: Thou hast beheld that the book proceeded forth from the mouth of a Jew; and when it proceeded forth from the mouth of a Jew it contained the plainness of the gospel of the Lord, of whom the twelve apostles bear record; and they bear record according to the truth which is in the Lamb of God.

"Wherefore, these things go forth from the Jews in purity unto the Gentiles, according to the truth which is in God.

"And after they go forth by the hand of the twelve apostles of the Lamb, from the Jews unto the Gentiles, thou seest the foundation of a great and abominable church, which is most abominable above all other churches; for behold, they have taken away from the gospel of the Lamb many parts which are plain and most precious; and also many covenants of the Lord have they taken away.

"And all this have they done that they might pervert the right ways of the Lord, that they might blind the eyes and harden the hearts of the children of men.

"Wherefore, thou seest that after the book hath gone forth through the hands of the great and abominable church, that there are many plain and precious things taken away from the book, which is the book of the Lamb of God.

"And after these plain and precious things were taken away it goeth forth unto all the nations of the Gentiles; and after it goeth forth unto all the nations of the Gentiles, yea, even across the many waters which thou hast seen with the Gentiles which have gone forth out of captivity, thou seest—because of the many plain and precious things which have been taken out of the book, which were plain unto the understanding of the children of men, according to the plainness which is in the Lamb of God—because of these things which are taken away out of the gospel of the Lamb, an exceeding great many do stumble, yea, insomuch that Satan hath great power over them." (1 Nephi 13:20-29.)

And what is the book? It is the Holy Bible, the record of the people or stick of Judah.

But what is the record of the stick, or people, of Joseph? It is the Book of Mormon! The Lord so designates it. It is the record of the "stick" or nation of Joseph, and may be spoken of as a stick itself.

"Behold, this is wisdom in me; wherefore, marvel not, for the hour cometh that I will drink of the fruit of the vine with you on the earth, and with Moroni, whom I have sent unto you to reveal the Book of Mormon, containing the fulness of my everlasting gospel, to whom I have committed the keys of the record of the stick of Ephraim." (D&C 27:5.)

Part of the gathering of Israel in the last days will be the uniting of these two volumes of scripture, so that they will be as one in the hands of the Lord's people.

Joseph who was sold into Egypt became a great prophet. He spoke of the reuniting of the tribes of Israel, but he also told of the coming together of their writings. Lehi read the words of Joseph as they were inscribed on the brass plates. The Lord spoke to Joseph and said:

"Wherefore, the fruit of thy loins shall write; and the fruit of the loins of Judah shall write; and that which shall be written by the fruit of thy loins, and also that which shall be written by the fruit of the loins of Judah, shall grow together, unto the confounding of false doctrines and laying down of contentions, and establishing peace among the fruit of thy loins, and bringing them to the knowledge of their fathers in the latter days, and also to the knowledge of my covenants, saith the Lord." (2 Nephi 3:12.)

Again we have a prophecy of the two volumes of scripture coming together. And again we see that it was to be a part of the gathering of Israel.

As the sticks are joined into one, the Lord tells of the blessings he will give to the gathered tribes:

"And they shall cry from the dust; yea, even repentance unto their brethren, even after many generations have gone by them. And it shall come to pass that their cry shall go, even according to the simpleness of their words.

"Because of their faith their words shall proceed forth out of my mouth unto their brethren who are the fruit of thy loins; and the weakness of their words will I make strong in their faith, unto the remembering of my covenant which I made unto thy fathers.

"And now, behold, my son Joseph, after this manner did my father of old prophesy.

"Wherefore, because of this covenant thou art blessed; for thy seed shall not be destroyed, for they shall hearken unto the words of the book.

"And there shall rise up one mighty among them, who shall do much good, both in word and in deed, being an instrument in the hands of God, with exceeding faith, to work mighty wonders, and do that thing which is great in the sight of God, unto the bringing to pass much restoration unto the house of Israel, and unto the seed of thy brethren.

"And now, blessed art thou, Joseph. Behold, thou art

little; wherefore hearken unto the words of thy brother, Nephi, and it shall be done unto thee even according to the words which I have spoken. Remember the words of thy dying father. Amen." (2 Nephi 3:20-25.)

As we read Ezekiel, it becomes evident that the joining of the two volumes of scripture is literally to be part and parcel of the final gathering. That drama is well underway. Three million Jews are now in Palestine establishing their homeland. To that homeland millions more will go eventually, including the ten lost tribes who will first come to Ephraim to receive their priesthood blessings, after which they will move on to Palestine, which is given to them as an inheritance. (D&C 133:26-34.)

Ephraim is being gathered from the four quarters of the earth. Salt Lake City is the present headquarters for this movement. Eventually the Lord will reign from the Zion to be built in Jackson County, but he will speak also from the Old Jerusalem when that city is restored. Then will come the fulfillment of the testimony of Isaiah:

"Out of Zion shall go forth the law, and the word of the Lord from Jerusalem." (Isaiah 2:3.)

Chapter Twenty-seven

JESUS AND ISAIAH

The Savior and the New Testament writers quoted more from Isaiah than from any other prophet except Moses. This is significant.

It was the Lord who said, "Great are the words of Isaiah," and he showed his evaluation by his use of those words, both in the Bible and in the Book of Mormon.

Esaias, or Isaiah, is quoted thirteen times in the four Gospels, and eight additional times elsewhere in the New Testament.

Matthew refers to the prophecy of Esaias concerning John the Baptist: "For this is he that was spoken of by the prophet Esaias, saying, The voice of one crying in the wilderness, Prepare ye the way of the Lord, make his paths straight." (Matthew 3:3. See also Isaiah 40:3.)

This is mentioned also in Luke: "As it is written in the book of the words of Esaias the prophet, saying, The voice of one crying in the wilderness, Prepare ye the way of the Lord, make his paths straight." (Luke 3:4.)

The Gospel of John quotes John the Baptist as identifying himself, from the words of Isaiah, as the voice of one crying in the wilderness. This passage reads:

"And this is the record of John, when the Jews sent priests and Levites from Jerusalem to ask him, Who art thou?

"And he confessed, and denied not; but confessed, I am not the Christ.

"And they asked him, What then? Art thou Elias? And he saith, I am not. Art thou that prophet? And he answered, No.

"Then said they unto him, Who art thou? that we

may give an answer to them that sent us. What sayest thou of thyself?

"He said, I am the voice of one crying in the wilderness, Make straight the way of the Lord, as said the prophet Esaias." (John 1:19-23.)

Again in reference to John the Baptist, it is seen that Isaiah also predicted the coming of the Messiah whose forerunner John would be.

On one occasion Jesus went to Capernaum on the borders of Zabulon and Nephthalim, and Matthew points out that it was a fulfillment of another of Isaiah's prophecies: "That it might be fulfilled which was spoken by Esaias the prophet, saying, The land of Zabulon, and the land of Nephthalim, by the way of the sea, beyond Jordan, Galilee of the Gentiles; the people which sat in darkness saw great light; and to them which sat in the region and shadow of death light is sprung up." (Matthew 4:14-16. See also Isaiah 9:1-2.)

The *light,* of course, was the gospel that Christ himself had brought to the people. Here again Isaiah predicted details concerning the ministry of the Savior.

Matthew referred once more to Isaiah when he wrote: "When the even was come, they brought unto him many that were possessed with devils: and he cast out the spirits with his word, and healed all that were sick: That it might be fulfilled which was spoken by Esaias the prophet saying, Himself took our infirmities, and bare our sicknesses." (Matthew 8:16-17. See also Isaiah 53:4.)

Again, it is evident that Isaiah gave advance details on the Savior's ministry.

When the Pharisees sought to destroy the Lord, Matthew writes, Jesus "withdrew himself from thence: and great multitudes followed him, and he healed them all; and charged them that they should not make him known: That it might be fulfilled which was spoken by Esaias the prophet, saying, Behold my servant, whom I have chosen; my beloved, in whom my soul is well pleased: I will put my spirit upon him, and he shall shew judgment to the Gentiles.'' (Matthew 12:14-18. See also Isaiah 42:1-3.)

In explaining his parables to his disciples, the Savior said:

''Because it is given unto you to know the mysteries of the kingdom of heaven, but to them it is not given. For whosoever hath, to him shall be given, and he shall have more abundance: but whosoever hath not, from him shall be taken away even that he hath. Therefore speak I to them in parables: because they seeing see not; and hearing they hear not, neither do they understand.

''And in them is fulfilled the prophecy of Esaias, which saith, By hearing ye shall hear, and shall not understand; and seeing ye shall see, and shall not perceive: For this people's heart is waxed gross, and their ears are dull of hearing, and their eyes they have closed; lest at any time they should see with their eyes, and hear with their ears, and should understand with their heart, and should be converted, and I should heal them.'' (Matthew 13:10-15. See also Isaiah 6:9-10.)

In one of his most piercing statements about unbelievers who follow false creeds, the Savior again quoted Isaiah. He had been assailed by the Pharisees concerning some of their traditions, and said:

''Why do ye also transgress the commandment of God by your tradition? . . . Ye hypocrites, well did Esaias prophesy of you, saying, This people draweth nigh unto me with their mouth, and honoureth me with their lips; but their heart is far from me. But in vain they do worship me, teaching for doctrines the commandments of men.'' (Matthew 15:3, 7-9. See also Isaiah 8:20; 29:13.)

This episode is referred to in the Gospel of Mark: ''Then the Pharisees and scribes asked him, Why walk not thy disciples according to the tradition of the elders, but eat bread with unwashen hands? He answered and said unto them, Well hath Esaias prophesied of you hypocrites, as it is written, This people honoureth me with their lips, but their heart is far from me. Howbeit in vain do they worship me, teaching for doctrines the commandments of men.'' (Mark 7:5-7.)

It was from the book of Isaiah that the Savior read while in the synagogue in Nazareth, raising resentment in the hearts of his listeners:

''And he came to Nazareth, where he had been brought up: and, as his custom was, he went into the synagogue on the sabbath day, and stood up for to read.

''And there was delivered unto him the book of the prophet Esaias. And when he had opened the book, he found the place where it was written,

''The Spirit of the Lord is upon me, because he hath anointed me to preach the gospel to the poor; he hath sent me to heal the brokenhearted, to preach deliverance to the captives, and recovering of sight to the blind, to set at liberty them that are bruised, to preach the acceptable year of the Lord.

''And he closed the book, and he gave it again to the minister, and sat down. And the eyes of all them that were in the synagogue were fastened on him.

''And he began to say unto them, This day is this scripture fulfilled in your ears.'' (Luke 4:16-21. See also Isaiah 61:1-2.)

John quoted Isaiah concerning the Savior's ministry:

''But though he had done so many miracles before them, yet they believed not on him: That the saying of Esaias the prophet might be fulfilled, which he spake, Lord, who hath believed our report? and to whom hath the arm of the Lord been revealed?

''Therefore they could not believe, because that Esaias said again, He hath blinded their eyes, and hardened their heart; that they should not see with their eyes, nor understand with their heart, and be converted, and I should heal them.

''These things said Esaias, when he saw his glory, and spake of him.'' (John 12:37-41. See also Isaiah 6:1-10; 53:1.)

The last sentence in the above quotation is significant. Could this be the same vision Isaiah saw in the year that King Uzziah died, or was this another glorious event? The scripture does not make it clear. But it is certain that Isaiah did see the Deity and that he evidently was well aware of Christ.

It was from Isaiah that the eunuch was reading when he was met by Philip, who converted him. (Acts 8:27-39.)

The fact that Isaiah possessed the gift of the Holy Ghost is taught by the apostle Paul: "And when they agreed not among themselves, they departed, after that Paul had spoken one word, Well spake the Holy Ghost by Esaias the prophet unto our fathers." (Acts 28:25.)

This recalls also the words of Isaiah concerning the Savior: "Hearken unto me, O Jacob and Israel, my called; I am he; I am the first, I also am the last. Mine hand also hath laid the foundation of the earth, and my right hand hath spanned the heavens: when I call unto them, they stand up together. . . .

"Come ye near unto me, hear ye this; I have not spoken in secret from the beginning; from the time that it was, there am I: and now the Lord God, and his Spirit, hath sent me. Thus saith the Lord, thy Redeemer, the Holy One of Israel; I am the Lord thy God which teacheth thee to profit, which leadeth thee by the way that thou shouldest go." (Isaiah 48:12-13, 16-17.)

Not only is this another affirmation of the Savior on the part of the Isaiah, but it also indicates the influence of the Holy Spirit which "hath sent me."

That the ancient prophets were moved by the power of the Holy Ghost is firmly declared by the apostle Peter: "Knowing this first, that no prophecy of the scripture is of any private interpretation. For the prophecy came not in old time by the will of man: but holy men of God spake as they were moved by the Holy Ghost." (2 Peter 1:20-21.)

Jesus was the Jehovah of the Old Testament, just as he was Christ of the New. Since he was the Creator, his ministry encompassed the entire time period of this earth.

Those who say that there was no evidence of the Trinity in the Godhead in Old Testament times simply do not have all of the facts. The Father, Son, and Holy Ghost have labored with and for this earth from its beginning and will do so until the end. Through the ages they used prophets whom they had appointed on earth, and Isaiah was one of the greatest of them.

Chapter Twenty-eight

TEACHINGS OF JESUS

When the Savior ministered among the Nephites, he taught them many things concerning the latter days and the gathering of Israel, in addition to other principles of the gospel. He quoted Isaiah in doing so.

He gave them the Sermon on the Mount. He explained that he himself was the God of the Old Testament, and that his gospel now superseded the law of Moses. And he informed the Nephites that it was he who gave the law to Moses.

"I am he that gave the law, and I am he who covenanted with my people Israel," he told them. "I have come to fulfill the law; therefore it hath an end." The gospel in its fulness was to take its place. "Behold, I do not destroy the prophets, for as many as have not been fulfilled in me, verily I say unto you, shall all be fulfilled." (3 Nephi 15:5-6.)

He had chosen his Twelve by this time, and said to them, "Ye are my disciples and ye are a light unto this people, who are a remnant of the house of Joseph." (3 Nephi 15:12.)

He gave the land of America to the house of Joseph for their special inheritance. "Behold, this is the land of your inheritance; and the Father hath given it unto you," he told the Nephites. (3 Nephi 15:13.)

It is noteworthy to see how closely the Father was associated with his Beloved Son in the work. It was the Father who gave America to Joseph, the Lord said, taking no credit to himself. The Savior told the Nephites also that they were the "other sheep" mentioned in the tenth chapter of John. Again he said that it was the Father who had instructed that he should tell the Nephites of this fact.

"And now, because of stiffneckedness and unbelief they understood not my word; therefore I was commanded to say no more of the Father concerning this thing unto them.

"But, verily, I say unto you that the Father hath commanded me, and I tell it unto you, that ye were separated from among them because of their iniquity; therefore it is because of their iniquity that they know not of you.

"And verily, I say unto you again that the other tribes hath the Father separated from them; and it is because of their iniquity that they know not of them.

"And verily I say unto you, that ye are they of whom I said: Other sheep I have which are not of this fold; them also I must bring, and they shall hear my voice; and there shall be one fold, and one shepherd.

"And they understood me not, for they supposed it had been the Gentiles; for they understood not that the Gentiles should be converted through their preaching.

"And they understood me not that I said they shall hear my voice; and they understood me not that the Gentiles should not at any time hear my voice—that I should not manifest myself unto them save it were by the Holy Ghost.

"But behold, ye have both heard my voice, and seen me; and ye are my sheep, and ye are numbered among those whom the Father hath given me." (3 Nephi 15:18-24.)

Note the honor the Savior pays to his Father. Note the fact that it is the Father giving directions for mankind, but doing so through the agency of Jesus. This fits into the pattern as expressed elsewhere too. The apostle Paul said that all creation was made by Jesus as the agent of the Father:

"God, who at sundry times and in divers manners spake in time past unto the fathers by the prophets, hath in these last days spoken unto us by his Son, whom he hath appointed heir of all things, by whom also he made the worlds; Who being the brightness of his glory, and the express image of his person, and upholding all things by the word of his power, when he had by himself purged our sins, sat down on the right hand of the Majesty on high." (Hebrews 1:1-3.)

Paul taught the same doctrine to the Colossians when he wrote:

"Giving thanks unto the Father, which hath made us meet to be partakers of the inheritance of the saints in light: Who hath delivered us from the power of darkness, and hath translated us into the kingdom of his dear Son: In whom we have redemption through his blood, even the forgiveness of sins: Who is the image of the invisible God, the firstborn of every creature:

"For by him were all things created, that are in heaven, and that are in earth, visible and invisible, whether they be thrones, or dominions, or principalities, or powers: all things were created by him, and for him: And he is before all things, and by him all things consist. And he is the head of the body, the church: who is the beginning, the firstborn from the dead; that in all things he might have the preeminence. For it pleased the Father that in him should all fulness dwell." (Colossians 1:12-19.)

In the Pearl of Great Price we again learn that the Father created all things through the agency of his Son: "And by the word of my power, have I created them, which is mine Only Begotten Son, who is full of grace and truth. And worlds without number have I created; and I also created them for mine own purpose; and by the Son I created them, which is mine Only Begotten." (Moses 1:32-33.)

The close relationship of the Father and the Son should never be forgotten. Many incidents in the life of the Savior illustrate this fact. For example, recall the raising of Lazarus. Before doing so, the Savior "lifted up his eyes and said, Father, I thank thee that thou hast heard me." (John 11:41.) He did not attempt to raise

Lazarus on his own responsibility. He recognized the Father.

So did not the Father and the Son cooperate in the closest kind of relationship? This we must recognize. It helps us to understand the Savior better. It helps us to know why it is that Jesus instructed us to pray not to himself, although he is the Redeemer, but to the Father, in the name of Jesus. Always the Father comes first. We are to become like the Father (see Matthew 5:48), but through Jesus the Savior.

This great principle the Lord taught to the Nephites.

He then turned to the events of latter days. He spoke of the gospel going to the Gentiles and said that if they will repent "and return unto me, saith the Father, behold they shall be numbered among my people, O house of Israel." (3 Nephi 16:13.)

It was at this point that the Lord quoted Isaiah concerning these last days:

"Verily, verily, I say unto you, thus hath the Father commanded me—that I should give unto this people this land for their inheritance.

"And then the words of the prophet Isaiah shall be fulfilled, which say: Thy watchmen shall lift up the voice; with the voice together shall they sing, for they shall see eye to eye when the Lord shall bring again Zion.

"Break forth into joy, sing together, ye waste places of Jerusalem; for the Lord hath comforted his people, he hath redeemed Jerusalem. The Lord hath made bare his holy arm in the eye of all the nations; and all the ends of the earth shall see the salvation of God." (3 Nephi 16:16-20. See also Isaiah 52:8-10.)

He also told them:

"Ye remember that I spake unto you, and said that when the words of Isaiah should be fulfilled—behold they are written, ye have them before you, therefore search them—And verily, verily, I say unto you, that when they shall be fulfilled then is the fulfilling of the covenant which the Father hath made unto his people, O house of Israel.

"And then shall the remnants, which shall be scattered abroad upon the face of the earth, be gathered in from the east and from the west, and from the south and from the north; and they shall be brought to the knowledge of the Lord their God, who hath redeemed them." (3 Nephi 20:11-13.)

Following this the Lord quoted an entire chapter from Isaiah, further expressing his love for Israel and promising millennial peace. We quote only a part: "For a small moment have I forsaken thee, but with great mercies will I gather thee. In a little wrath I hid my face from thee for a moment, but with everlasting kindness will I have mercy on thee, saith the Lord thy Redeemer. . . . For the mountains shall depart and the hills be removed, but my kindness shall not depart from thee, neither shall the covenant of my people be removed, saith the Lord that hath mercy on thee." (3 Nephi 22:7-8, 10. See also Isaiah 54:7-8, 10.)

The fact that the Savior would quote Isaiah in this manner has much significance. He had given the same information to that prophet seven hundred years before, even as he now gave it to the Nephites.

Here is an amazing fact. The Third Nephi statement given by the Savior in direct instruction to the Nephites is almost identical to the King James version of this scripture. The Savior thus once more emphasized that "great are the words of Isaiah." By using them, he verified their accuracy and that of the King James Version as well.

Some scholars attempt to cheapen the Savior's sermon by saying that Joseph Smith wrote it himself, borrowing language from the King James Version of the Bible and inserting it into the Lord's address to the Nephites. The Book of Mormon is a complete translation of the ancient record, and in no sense is it a composition of Joseph Smith.

The Savior's sermon, with its inclusion of the words of Isaiah, is of such superior quality that it is beyond the ability of mortal man. Joseph provides this classic utterance of the Savior strictly as a translation of the Lord's own words. It was possible only because Joseph translated by the power of God, and not by any of the very limited powers he possessed.

Jesus acknowledged Isaiah's greatness by incorporating into his own sermon the words found in Isaiah 54.

As for Isaiah, he was merely the spokesman of the Lord in his day. The words were those of Jehovah. Does Isaiah not give credit to the Lord for them, as he declares "saith the Lord" at several points in the chapter?

To Isaiah it was revelation, just as the sections in the Doctrine and Covenants were revealed to Joseph Smith, who took no credit for them himself. On this point he and Isaiah followed the same pattern.

Chapter Twenty-nine

SCATTERED ISRAEL

Isaiah foretold the scattering of Israel and the cruel manner in which it would be accomplished. But he also saw the eventual gathering of the tribes and the blessings that would come to them. One of his most notable prophecies on this subject reads:

"And it shall come to pass in that day, that the Lord shall set his hand again the second time to recover the remnant of his people, which shall be left, from Assyria, and from Egypt, and from Pathros, and from Cush, and from Elam, and from Shinar, and from Hamath, and from the islands of the sea.

"And he shall set up an ensign for the nations, and shall assemble the outcasts of Israel, and gather together the dispersed of Judah from the four corners of the earth." (Isaiah 11:11-12.)

Another was this, indicating the tender mercy of the Lord:

"For the Lord will have mercy on Jacob, and will yet choose Israel, and set them in their own land: and the strangers shall be joined with them, and they shall cleave to the house of Jacob.

"And the people shall take them, and bring them to their place: and the house of Israel shall possess them in the land of the Lord for servants and handmaids: and they shall take them captives, whose captives they were; and they shall rule over their oppressors.

"And it shall come to pass in the day that the Lord shall give thee rest from thy sorrow, and from thy fear, and from the hard bondage wherein thou wast made to serve." (Isaiah 14:1-3.)

He also said:

"The wilderness and the solitary place shall be glad for them; and the desert shall rejoice, and blossom as the rose.

"It shall blossom abundantly, and rejoice even with joy and singing; the glory of Lebanon shall be given unto it, the excellency of Carmel and Sharon, they shall see the glory of the Lord, and the excellency of our God.

"Strengthen ye the weak hands, and confirm the feeble knees.

"Say to them that are of a fearful heart, Be strong, fear not: behold, your God will come with vengeance, even God with a recompence; he will come and save you.

"Then the eyes of the blind shall be opened, and the ears of the deaf shall be unstopped.

"Then shall the lame man leap as an hart, and the tongue of the dumb sing: for in the wilderness shall waters break out, and streams in the desert.

"And the parched ground shall become a pool, and the thirsty land springs of water: in the habitation of dragons, where each lay, shall be grass with reeds and rushes.

"And an highway shall be there, and a way, and it shall be called The way of holiness; the unclean shall not pass over it; but it shall be for those: the wayfaring men, though fools, shall not err therein.

"No lion shall be there, nor any ravenous beast shall go up thereon, it shall not be found there; but the redeemed shall walk there:

"And the ransomed of the Lord shall return, and come to Zion with songs and everlasting joy upon their heads: they shall obtain joy and gladness, and sorrow and sighing shall flee away." (Isaiah 35.)

To allay their fears he added:

"Fear not: for I am with thee: I will bring thy seed from the east, and gather thee from the west; I will say to the north, Give up; and to the south, Keep not back: bring my sons from far, and my daughters from the ends

of the earth; even every one that is called by my name:
for I have created him for my glory, I have formed him;
yea, I have made him." (Isaiah 43:5-7.)

Lest they may think the Lord has abandoned his
people, Isaiah continues: "For a small moment I have
forsaken thee; but with great mercies will I gather thee.
In a little wrath I hid my face from thee for a moment; but
with everlasting kindness will I have mercy on thee, saith
the Lord thy Redeemer." (Isaiah 54:7-8.)

He describes what they will do in Palestine, much of
which has already been done by the industrious and
skillful Jews who now live there:

"And they shall build the old wastes, they shall raise
up the former desolations, and they shall repair the waste
cities, the desolations of many generations.

"And strangers shall stand and feed your flocks, and
the sons of the alien shall be your plowmen and your
vinedressers.

"But ye shall be named the Priests of the Lord: men
shall call you the Ministers of our God: ye shall eat the
riches of the Gentiles, and in their glory shall ye boast
yourselves." (Isaiah 61:4-6.)

And he said: "For the Lord shall comfort Zion: he
will comfort all her waste places; and he will make her
wilderness like Eden, and her desert like the garden of
the Lord; joy and gladness shall be found therein,
thanksgiving, and the voice of melody. . . . Therefore the
redeemed of the Lord shall return, and come with singing
unto Zion; and everlasting joy shall be upon their head:
they shall obtain gladness and joy; and sorrow and
mourning shall flee away." (Isaiah 51:3, 11.)

Chapter Thirty

THE OLD JERUSALEM

A mighty drama will be enacted at the Old Jerusalem both before and after the second coming of the Lord.

The present gathering of the Jews to that land is itself a fulfillment of ancient prophecies. Palestine indeed has been made to blossom as the rose. But it will be a target for oppressors in the latter days, those "who seek a prey." It was Ezekiel who wrote the detail of the siege of Jerusalem to take place before the coming of the Lord. He saw the armies of a mighty northern nation surrounding the city.

"Persia, Ethiopia, and Libya with them; all of them with shield and helmet: Gomer, and all his bands; the house of Togarmah of the north quarters, and all his bands: and many people with thee.

"Be thou prepared, and prepare for thyself, thou, and all thy company that are assembled unto thee, and be thou a guard unto them.

"After many days thou shalt be visited: in the latter years thou shalt come into the land that is brought back from the sword, and is gathered out of many people, against the mountains of Israel, which have been always waste: but it is brought forth out of the nations, and they shall dwell safely all of them.

"Thou shalt ascend and come like a storm, thou shalt be like a cloud to cover the land, thou, and all thy bands, and many people with thee.

"Thus saith the Lord God; It shall also come to pass, that at the same time shall things come into thy mind, and thou shalt think an evil thought:

"And thou shalt say, I will go up to the land of

unwalled villages; I will go to them that are at rest, that dwell safely, all of them dwelling without walls, and having neither bars nor gates,

"To take a spoil, and to take a prey; to turn thine hand upon the desolate places that are now inhabited, and upon the people that are gathered out of the nations, which have gotten cattle and goods, that dwell in the midst of the land.

"Sheba, and Dedan, and the merchants of Tarshish, with all the young lions thereof, shall say unto thee, Art thou come to take a spoil? hast thou gathered thy company to take a prey? to carry away silver and gold, to take away cattle and goods, to take a great spoil?

"Therefore, son of man, prophesy and say unto Gog, Thus saith the Lord God; In that day when my people of Israel dwelleth safely, shalt thou not know it?

"And thou shalt come from thy place out of the north parts, thou, and many people with thee, all of them riding upon horses, a great company, and a mighty army:

"And thou shalt come up against my people of Israel, as a cloud to cover the land; it shall be in the latter days, and I will bring thee against my land, that the heathen may know me, when I shall be sanctified in thee, O Gog, before their eyes." (Ezekiel 38:5-16.)

In the midst of the war, the Lord will come to the rescue of his people. As the enemy invades their land and besieges their city, destroying a large part of it, the Jews will flee toward the Mount of Olives.

"Then shall the arm of the Lord fall upon the nations. And then shall the Lord set his foot upon this mount, and it shall cleave in twain, and the earth shall tremble, and reel to and fro, and the heavens also shall shake.

"And the Lord shall utter his voice, and all the ends of the earth shall hear it; and the nations of the earth shall mourn, and they that have laughed shall see their folly. And calamity shall cover the mocker, and the scorner shall be consumed; and they that have watched for iniquity shall be hewn down and cast into the fire.

"And then shall the Jews look upon me and say:

What are these wounds in thine hands and in thy feet?

"Then shall they know that I am the Lord; for I will say unto them: These wounds are the wounds with which I was wounded in the house of my friends. I am he who was lifted up. I am Jesus that was crucified. I am the Son of God.

"And then shall they weep because of their iniquities; then shall they lament because they persecuted their king. And then shall the heathen nations be redeemed, and they that knew no law shall have part in the first resurrection; and it shall be tolerable for them. And Satan shall be bound, that he shall have no place in the hearts of the children of men." (D&C 45:47-55.)

The destruction of the enemy forces will be great.

"And it shall be in that day, that living waters shall go out from Jerusalem; half of them toward the former sea, and half of them toward the hinder sea: in summer and in winter shall it be.

"And the Lord shall be king over all the earth: in that day shall there be one Lord, and his name one.

"All the land shall be turned as a plain from Geba to Rimmon south of Jerusalem: and it shall be lifted up, and inhabited in her place, from Benjamin's gate unto the place of the first gate, unto the corner gate, and from the tower of Hananeel unto the king's winepresses.

"And men shall dwell in it, and there shall be no more utter destruction; but Jerusalem shall be safely inhabited." (Zechariah 14:8-11.)

He then continues his further description of what will come to the Old Jerusalem:

"And it shall come to pass, that every one that is left of all the nations which came against Jerusalem shall even go up from year to year to worship the King, the Lord of hosts, and to keep the feast of tabernacles.

"And it shall be, that whoso will not come up of all the families of the earth unto Jerusalem to worship the King, the Lord of hosts, even upon them shall be no rain." (Zechariah 14:16-17.)

One of the events that will affect both the Old and the

New Jerusalem will be the return of the lost Ten Tribes. Of that, modern revelation says:

"Wherefore, prepare ye for the coming of the Bridegroom; go ye, go ye out to meet him.

"For behold, he shall stand upon the mount of Olivet, and upon the mighty ocean, even the great deep, and upon the islands of the sea, and upon the land of Zion. And he shall utter his voice out of Zion, and he shall speak from Jerusalem, and his voice shall be heard among all people; and it shall be a voice as the voice of many waters, and as the voice of a great thunder, which shall break down the mountains, and the valleys shall not be found.

"He shall command the great deep, and it shall be driven back into the north countries, and the islands shall become one land; and the land of Jerusalem and the land of Zion shall be turned back into their own place, and the earth shall be like it was in the days before it was divided.

"And the Lord, even the Savior, shall stand in the midst of his people, and shall reign over all flesh.

"And they who are in the north countries shall come in remembrance before the Lord; and their prophets shall hear his voice, and shall no longer stay themselves; and they shall smite the rocks, and the ice shall flow down at their presence.

"And an highway shall be cast up in the midst of the great deep.

"Their enemies shall become a prey unto them, and in the barren deserts there shall come forth pools of living water; and the parched ground shall no longer be a thirsty land.

"And they shall bring forth their rich treasures unto the children of Ephraim, my servants.

"And the boundaries of the everlasting hills shall tremble at their presence. And there shall they fall down and be crowned with glory, even in Zion, by the hands of the servants of the Lord, even the children of Ephraim. And they shall be filled with songs of everlasting joy.

"Behold, this is the blessing of the everlasting God upon the tribes of Israel, and the richer blessing upon the head of Ephraim and his fellows. And they also of the tribe of Judah, after their pain shall be sanctified in holiness before the Lord, to dwell in his presence day and night, forever and ever." (D&C 133:19-35.)

And then Isaiah concludes:

"In that day shall the branch of the Lord be beautiful and glorious, and the fruit of the earth shall be excellent and comely for them that are escaped of Israel.

"And it shall come to pass, that he that is left in Zion, and he that remaineth in Jerusalem, shall be called holy, even every one that is written among the living in Jerusalem:

"When the Lord shall have washed away the filth of the daughters of Zion, and shall have purged the blood of Jerusalem from the midst thereof by the spirit of judgment, and by the spirit of burning.

"And the Lord will create upon every dwelling place of mount Zion, and upon her assemblies, a cloud and smoke by day, and the shining of a flaming fire by night: for upon all the glory shall be a defence.

"And there shall be a tabernacle for a shadow in the daytime from the heat, and for a place of refuge, and for a covert from storm and from rain." (Isaiah 4:2-6.)

Chapter Thirty-one

WHO WROTE ISAIAH?

For years controversy has raged among Bible scholars as to whether or not the Book of Isaiah had more than one author. Some say there were at least two, separated by as much as two hundred years. Others think there were three.

An alleged difference in writing styles is one of the reasons for their suppositions. However, some claim that the treatment of historical facts precludes the entire book from having been written by one person in the time period of about 720 B.C.

Certain events are mentioned in some of the chapters as having already taken place, whereas they happened two centuries after it is known that Isaiah lived. On this point the *Encyclopaedia Judaica* (9:46) says: "The virtually unanimous opinion in modern times is that Isaiah is to be considered the work of two distinct authors: First Isaiah (chs. 1-39) whose prophetic career in Jerusalem covers the years c. 740–700 B.C.E., and that of an unknown prophet (Deutero-Isaiah, chs. 40-66) whose prophecies reflect the experience and events of the Babylonian Exile (c. 540 B.C.E.)."

The same authority, however, says that Jewish scholars do not agree with this claim. They hold to a single authorship. Says the *Judaica* (9:44): "It was generally axiomatic among the rabbis that the Book of Isaiah was the work of one prophet, and they answered the apparent time discrepancy by attributing the latter chapters to the outcome of prophetic powers." Abinadi did the same thing in the Book of Mormon. (See Mosiah 15, for example.)

In modern revelation no suggestion of more than one author appears. The writings of Isaiah are identified with but one expression—"the words of Isaiah"—regardless of whether the early or the later chapters are used.

For example, the Savior quoted Isaiah 52, one of the later chapters, as he addressed the Nephites (3 Nephi 20:36-46) without raising the question of authorship.

The same thing is true of the Lord's sermon as recorded in Third Nephi 22, quoting Isaiah 54. As part of that sermon the Lord said: "A commandment I give unto you that ye search these things diligently; for great are the words of Isaiah." (3 Nephi 23:1.) Thus he refers to chapter 54, one of the later ones in the book, and which Jesus identified as Isaiah's work.

He did not teach us to search the words of the first Isaiah or the second Isaiah or the third Isaiah. He quoted Isaiah as we have it in the King James Version, and commanded us "to search *these things* diligently; for great are the words of Isaiah." He clearly identified "these things" as the work of Isaiah. Is there a better authority?

When Moroni wrote "Search the prophecies of Isaiah" (Mormon 8:23), he did not quibble over authorship. It was Isaiah of whom he spoke, and there is only one *known* Isaiah, despite speculation to the contrary.

The first Nephi in the Book of Mormon quoted generously from Isaiah and specifically identified his quotations as coming from that prophet. There was no question in his mind as to whether there was more than one author. He spoke of Isaiah the prophet, and there is only one prophet known by that name.

When the Lord gave us section 113 of the Doctrine and Covenants, answering questions about Isaiah, nothing was said challenging the authorship that appeared under that name. Isaiah was the prophet. No question was raised as to authorship—not by the Lord.

When the Lord gave us section 76 of the Doctrine and

Covenants, he included this passage in explanation of the glory of the telestial world:

"And the glory of the telestial is one, even as the glory of the stars is one; for as one star differs from another star in glory, even so differs one from another in glory in the telestial world;

"For these are they who are of Paul, and of Apollos, and of Cephas.

"These are they who say they are some of one and some of another—some of Christ and some of John, and some of Moses, and some of Elias, and some of Esaias, and some of Isaiah, and some of Enoch." (D&C 76:98-100.)

Again no question is raised in modern revelation about the identity of Isaiah.

Latter-day Saints need not worry about the authorship of the book of Isaiah. If there had been question about either it or the veracity of its contents, would not the Lord have told us?

He did not hesitate to discuss the Apochrypha, and he cautioned us against that book. (D&C 91.) If there was anything apochryphal about Isaiah, we surely would have been told in the same way. But on the contrary, the Book of Mormon prophets and the Savior himself freely quoted from Isaiah without reservation, thus recommending and endorsing what was written under that name.

When the Lord said "great are the words of Isaiah," he spoke of only one man, and his references include scriptures from both the early and the latter part of Isaiah's book, which is particularly pertinent to this point.

Chapter Thirty-two

ISAIAH AS A POET

The quality of Isaiah's writing exceeds most of the literature now in print, either modern or ancient. No uninspired writers even approach him. Most of his work is poetic, although much of it is in direct prose. The prose is forceful, the style dynamic, the language superb.

Who can read such masterpieces as chapter 53 of Isaiah and not realize that the Holy Spirit guided him, that he was poetic in very deed, but that he was a prophet above all else?

The sheer beauty of his language is impressive, made infinitely more so by the message. Says the prophet concerning Jesus:

He is despised and rejected of men;
A man of sorrows, and acquainted with grief:
And we hid as it were our faces from him;
He was despised, and we esteemed him not.
Surely he hath borne our griefs,
And carried our sorrows:
Yet we did esteem him stricken,
Smitten of God, and afflicted.

But he was wounded for our transgressions,
He was bruised for our iniquities:
The chastisement of our peace was upon him;
And with his stripes we are healed.

All we like sheep have gone astray;
We have turned every one to his own way;
And the Lord hath laid on him
The iniquity of us all.
—Isaiah 53:3-6

And no poetry can exceed these words:

How beautiful upon the mountains
        Are the feet of him
That bringeth good tidings,
        that publisheth peace;
That bringeth good tidings of good,
        That publisheth salvation;
That saith unto Zion,
        Thy God reigneth!

Break forth into joy, sing together,
        Ye waste places of Jerusalem;
For the Lord hath comforted his people,
        He hath redeemed Jerusalem.
                —Isaiah 52:7, 9

An example of his straightforward rebukes appears in his third chapter. There he speaks of the judgment that will befall the unrepentant. He speaks to the daughters of Zion in particular and says:

"Moreover the Lord saith, Because the daughters of Zion are haughty, and walk with stretched forth necks and wanton eyes, walking and mincing as they go, and making a tinkling with their feet:

"Therefore the Lord will smite with a scab the crown of the head of the daughters of Zion, and the Lord will discover their secret parts.

"In that day the Lord will take away the bravery of their tinkling ornaments about their feet, and their cauls, and their round tires like the moon, the chains, and the bracelets, and the mufflers, the bonnets, and the ornaments of the legs, and the headbands, and the tablets, and the earrings, the rings, and nose jewels, the changeable suits of apparel, and the mantles, and the wimples, and the crisping pins, the glasses, and the fine linen, and the hoods, and the vails.

"And it shall come to pass, that instead of sweet smell there shall be stink; and instead of a girdle a rent;

and instead of well set hair baldness; and instead of a stomacher a girding of sackcloth; and burning instead of beauty.

"Thy men shall fall by the sword, and thy mighty in the war.

"And her gates shall lament and mourn; and she being desolate shall sit upon the ground." (Isaiah 3:16-26.)

His use of contrasts and comparisons is found in many parts of his book. One notable example is seen in chapter 28:

"Give ye ear, and hear my voice; hearken, and hear my speech.

"Doth the plowman plow all day to sow? doth he open and break the clods of his ground?

"When he hath made plain the face thereof, doth he not cast abroad the fitches, and scatter the cummin, and cast in the principal wheat and the appointed barley and the rie in their place?

"For his God doth instruct him to discretion, and doth teach him.

"For the fitches are not threshed with a threshing instrument, neither is a cart wheel turned about upon the cummin; but the fitches are beaten out with a staff, and the cummin with a rod.

"Bread corn is bruised; because he will not ever be threshing it, nor break it with the wheel of his cart, nor bruise it with his horsemen.

"This also cometh forth from the Lord of hosts, which is wonderful in counsel, and excellent in working." (Isaiah 28:23-29.)

His prayers are also eloquent:

"O Lord, be gracious unto us; we have waited for thee: be thou their arm every morning, our salvation also in the time of trouble.

"At the noise of the tumult the people fled; at the lifting up of thyself the nations were scattered. And your spoil shall be gathered like the gathering of the caterpiller: as the running to and fro of locusts shall he run upon them.

"The Lord is exalted; for he dwelleth on high: he hath filled Zion with judgment and righteousness. And wisdom and knowledge shall be the stablity of thy times, and strength of salvation: the fear of the Lord is his treasure.

"Behold, their valiant ones shall cry without: the ambassadors of peace shall weep bitterly.

"The highways lie waste, the wayfaring man ceaseth: he hath broken the covenant, he hath despised the cities, he regardeth no man." (Isaiah 33:2-8.)

In another appeal to the women of Israel he cries out:

"Rise up, ye women that are at ease; hear my voice, ye careless daughters; give ear unto my speech.

"Many days and years shall ye be troubled, ye careless women: for the vintage shall fail, the gathering shall not come.

"Tremble, ye women that are at ease; be troubled, ye careless ones: strip you, and make you bare, and gird sackcloth upon your loins. They shall lament for the teats, for the pleasant fields, for the fruitful vine.

"Upon the land of my people shall come up thorns and briers; yea, upon all the houses of joy in the joyous city: Because the palaces shall be forsaken; the multitude of the city shall be left; the forts and towers shall be for dens for ever, a joy of wild asses, a pasture of flocks;

"Until the spirit be poured upon us from on high, and the wilderness be a fruitful field, and the fruitful field be counted for a forest." (Isaiah 32:9-15.)

Isaiah, like David and Solomon, wrote under the inspiration of the Holy Spirit. Their day-to-day education, as it was, could in no way equip them to write so beautifully.

The same thing may be said of the Prophet Joseph Smith. It is true that he was not educated in the colleges of the world, but he was taught by the Holy Spirit.

On this point do we recall what was said of the Savior? "Now about the midst of the feast Jesus went up into the temple, and taught. And the Jews marvelled, saying, How knoweth this man letters, having never learned?'' (John 7:14-15.)

With all the great prophets, and especially those who wrote so beautifully, credit indeed must be given to the Lord for their majestic expressions. Sheer inspiration is the word for it.

Consider this from the Prophet Joseph Smith:

"Hearken, O ye people of my church, saith the voice of him who dwells on high, and whose eyes are upon all men; yea, verily I say: Hearken ye people from afar; and ye that are upon the islands of the sea, listen together.

"For verily the voice of the Lord is unto all men, and there is none to escape; and there is no eye that shall not see, neither ear that shall not hear, neither heart that shall not be penetrated.

"And the rebellious shall be pierced with much sorrow; for their iniquities shall be spoken upon the housetops, and their secret acts shall be revealed.

"And the voice of warning shall be unto all people, by the mouths of my disciples, whom I have chosen in these last days.

"And they shall go forth and none shall stay them, for I the Lord have commanded them." (D&C 1:1-5.)

Could an unlettered man have written that without divine help? Or could he have written this:

"Hear, O ye heavens, and give ear, O earth, and rejoice ye inhabitants thereof, for the Lord is God, and beside him there is no Savior.

"Great is his wisdom, marvelous are his ways, and the extent of his doings none can find out.

"His purposes fail not, neither are there any who can stay his hand.

"From eternity to eternity he is the same, and his years never fail.

"For thus saith the Lord—I, the Lord, am merciful and gracious unto those who fear me, and delight to honor those who serve me in righteousness and in truth unto the end. Great shall be their reward and eternal shall be their glory.

"And to them will I reveal all mysteries, yea, all the hidden mysteries of my kingdom from days of old, and for ages to come, will I make known unto them the good pleasure of my will concerning all things pertaining to my kingdom.

"Yea, even the wonders of eternity shall they know, and things to come will I show them, even the things of many generations.

"And their wisdom shall be great, and their understanding reach to heaven; and before them the wisdom of the wise shall perish, and the understanding of the prudent shall come to naught.

"For by my Spirit will I enlighten them, and by my power will I make known unto them the secrets of my will—yea, even those things which eye has not seen, nor ear heard, nor yet entered into the heart of man." (D&C 76:1-10.)

Or this:

"How long can rolling waters remain impure? What power shall stay the heavens? As well might man stretch forth his puny arm to stop the Missouri river in its decreed course, or to turn it up stream, as to hinder the Almighty from pouring down knowledge from heaven upon the heads of the Latter-day Saints.

"Behold, there are many called, but few are chosen. And why are they not chosen?

"Because their hearts are set so much upon the things of this world, and aspire to the honors of men, that they do not learn this one lesson—

"That the rights of the priesthood are inseparably connected with the powers of heaven, and that the powers of heaven cannot be controlled nor handled only upon the principles of righteousness.

"That they may be conferred upon us, it is true; but when we undertake to cover our sins, or to gratify our pride, our vain ambition, or to exercise control or dominion or compulsion upon the souls of the children of men, in any degree of unrighteousness, behold, the heavens withdraw themselves; the Spirit of the Lord is grieved; and when it is withdrawn, Amen to the priesthood or the authority of that man.

"Behold, ere he is aware, he is left unto himself, to kick against the pricks, to persecute the saints, and to fight against God.

"We have learned by sad experience that it is the nature and disposition of almost all men, as soon as they get a little authority, as they suppose, they will immediately begin to exercise unrighteous dominion.

"Hence many are called, but few are chosen." (D&C 121:33-40.)

The Psalms of David were prophetic, and hence inspired of the Holy Spirit. The Proverbs of Solomon were likewise scriptural. Such things come only from the Lord. Such inspiration is what makes men prophetic.

Isaiah was truly inspired of the Lord, and the beauty of his works testifies of it.

Chapter Thirty-three

WHAT ISAIAH TAUGHT

Righteousness and full acceptance of the Holy One of Israel were the predominant teachings of the prophet Isaiah.

These principles were all embracing; they included acceptance of the Lord before his birth as well as during his mortality, and are reflected in his great latter-day work.

The modern phase of the Lord's ministry would, of course, include the restoration of the gospel, the coming forth of the Book of Mormon, and the journey of the Saints to the Rocky Mountains. It will yet include the gathering of all the tribes of Israel and the establishment of Zion in America and the restored Jerusalem in Palestine.

But especially Isaiah emphasized the coming of the Holy One of Israel to judgment in the last days, after which a millennial reign will begin, when the lion and the lamb will lie down together and a sacred peace will descend upon the earth.

Included in his over-all message were many other teachings that deserve special mention. One of them was his charge to honor the Sabbath day. In his first chapter he demanded sincerity of the people and denounced them for hypocrisy, which must have included a mock observance of the Sabbath. Said he:

"Except the Lord of hosts had left unto us a very small remnant, we should have been as Sodom, and we should have been like unto Gomorrah.

"Hear the word of the Lord, ye rulers of Sodom; give ear unto the law of our God, ye people of Gomorrah.

"To what purpose is the multitude of your sacrifices unto me? saith the Lord: I am full of the burnt offerings of rams, and the fat of fed beasts; and I delight not in the blood of bullocks, or of lambs, or of he goats.

"When ye come to appear before me, who hath required this at your hand, to tread my courts?

"Bring no more vain oblations; incense is an abomination unto me; the new moons and sabbaths, the calling of assemblies, I cannot away with; it is iniquity, even the solemn meeting.

"Your new moons and your appointed feasts my soul hateth: they are a trouble unto me; I am weary to bear them.

"And when ye spread forth your hands, I will hide mine eyes from you: yea, when ye make many prayers, I will not hear: your hands are full of blood.

"Wash you, make you clean; put away the evil of your doings from before mine eyes; cease to do evil; learn to do well; seek judgment, relieve the oppressed, judge the fatherless, plead for the widow." (Isaiah 1:9-17.)

It was at this point that he taught one of his great lessons on repentance and the willingness of the Lord to accept honesty in worship: "Come now, and let us reason together, saith the Lord: though your sins be as scarlet, they shall be as white as snow; though they be red like crimson, they shall be as wool. If ye be willing and obedient, ye shall eat the good of the land: But if ye refuse and rebel, ye shall be devoured with the sword: for the mouth of the Lord hath spoken it." (Isaiah 1:18-20.)

He again mentioned the Sabbath as he called upon Israel at a later date to repent of all waywardness: "Blessed is the man that doeth this, and the son of man that layeth hold on it; that keepeth the sabbath from polluting it, and keepeth his hand from doing any evil. . . . Also the sons of the stranger, that join themselves to the Lord, to serve him, and to love the name of the Lord, to be his servants, every one that keepeth the sabbath from polluting it, and taketh hold of my covenant.'' (Isaiah 56:2, 6.)

With this great appeal he also said:

"Seek ye the Lord while he may be found, call ye upon him while he is near: Let the wicked forsake his way, and the unrighteous man his thoughts: and let him return unto the Lord, and he will have mercy upon him; and to our God, for he will abundantly pardon.

"For my thoughts are not your thoughts, neither are your ways my ways, saith the Lord. For as the heavens are higher than the earth, so are my ways higher than your ways, and my thoughts than your thoughts.'' (Isaiah 55:6-9.)

One of his most forceful expressions with regard to the Sabbath day is given in these words:

"If thou turn away thy foot from the sabbath, from doing thy pleasure on my holy day; and call the sabbath a delight, the holy of the Lord, honourable; and shalt honour him, not doing thine own ways, nor finding thine own pleasure, nor speaking thine own words:

"Then shalt thou delight thyself in the Lord; and I will cause thee to ride upon the high places of the earth, and feed thee with the heritage of Jacob thy father: for the mouth of the Lord hath spoken it.'' (Isaiah 58:13-14.)

And he continued with this: "Behold, the Lord's hand is not shortened, that it cannot save; neither his ear heavy, that it cannot hear: But your iniquities have separated between you and your God, and your sins have hid his face from you, that he will not hear.'' (Isaiah 59:1-2.)

He made many promises as rewards for obedience to the Lord. One of his choice expressions is this:

"Hast thou not known? hast thou not heard, that the everlasting God, the Lord, the Creator of the ends of the earth, fainteth not, neither is weary? there is no searching of his understanding.

"He giveth power to the faint; and to them that have no might he increaseth strength.

"Even the youths shall faint and be weary, and the young men shall utterly fall: But they that wait upon the Lord shall renew their strength; they shall mount up with wings as eagles; they shall run, and not be weary; and they shall walk, and not faint." (Isaiah 40:28-31.)

Another of his promises was this: "No weapon that is formed against thee shall prosper; and every tongue that shall rise against thee in judgment thou shalt condemn. This is the heritage of the servants of the Lord, and their righteousness is of me, saith the Lord." (Isaiah 54:17.)

As a warning against going into forbidden paths for light and guidance he said: "Through the wrath of the Lord of hosts is the land darkened, and the people shall be as the fuel of the fire: no man shall spare his brother. And he shall snatch on the right hand, and be hungry; and he shall eat on the left hand, and they shall not be satisfied: they shall eat every man the flesh of his own arm." (Isaiah 9:19-20.)

ISAIAH AND LUCIFER

As Isaiah battled idolatry, intrigue, and the influence of Assyria and Babylon that constantly undermined the character of his people, he knew full well the identity of his ultimate enemy.

He knew Lucifer and whence he had fallen. He brought this knowledge into his teachings also, trying to persuade his people to renounce the devil and all his emissaries. In describing Satan, Isaiah said:

"How art thou fallen from heaven, O Lucifer, son of the morning! how art thou cut down to the ground, which didst weaken the nations!

"For thou hast said in thine heart, I will ascend into heaven, I will exalt my throne above the stars of God: I will sit also upon the mount of the congregation, in the sides of the north:

"I will ascend above the heights of the clouds; I will be like the most High.

"Yet thou shalt be brought down to hell, to the sides of the pit.

"They that see thee shall narrowly look upon thee, and consider thee, saying, Is this the man that made the earth to tremble, that did shake kingdoms; That made the world as a wilderness, and destroyed the cities thereof; that opened not the house of his prisoners?

"All the kings of the nations, even all of them, like in glory, every one in his own house.

"But thou art cast out of thy grave like an abominable branch, and as the raiment of those that are slain, thrust through with a sword, that go down to the stones of the pit; as a carcase trodden under feet.

"Thou shalt not be joined with them in burial, because thou hast destroyed thy land, and slain thy people: the seed of evildoers shall never be renowned.'' (Isaiah 14:12-20.)

This recalls what John the Revelator wrote: ''And there was war in heaven: Michael and his angels fought against the dragon; and the dragon fought and his angels, and prevailed not; neither was their place found any more in heaven. And the great dragon was cast out, that old serpent, called the Devil, and Satan, which deceiveth the whole world: he was cast out into the earth, and his angels were cast out with him.'' (Revelation 12:7-9.)

This war in heaven began when Lucifer rebelled at the time Jehovah was chosen to be the Savior of the world. It is remembered that Moses wrote about him. Lucifer had appeared to Moses pretending to be the Savior, but Moses recognized his trickery and rebuked him, commanding him in the name of Christ to depart from him.

Then it was that ''the Lord God, spake unto Moses, saying: That Satan, whom thou hast commanded in the name of mine Only Begotten, is the same which was from the beginning, and he came before me, saying—Behold, here am I, send me, I will be thy son, and I will redeem all mankind, that one soul shall not be lost, and surely I will do it; wherefore give me thine honor.

''But, behold, my Beloved Son, which was my Beloved and Chosen from the beginning, said unto me—Father, thy will be done, and the glory be thine forever.

''Wherefore, because that Satan rebelled against me, and sought to destroy the agency of man, which I, the Lord God, had given him, and also, that I should give unto him mine own power; by the power of mine Only Begotten, I caused that he should be cast down;

''And he became Satan, yea, even the devil, the father of all lies, to deceive and to blind men, and to lead them captive at his will, even as many as would not hearken unto my voice.'' (Moses 4:1-4.)

Moses goes on to say that it was this same Satan, in the guise of a serpent, who tempted Adam and Eve in the

Garden of Eden. He continues with this interesting account:

"And Satan put it into the heart of the serpent, (for he had drawn away many after him,) and he sought also to beguile Eve, for he knew not the mind of God, wherefore he sought to destroy the world.

"And he said unto the woman: Yea, hath God said—Ye shall not eat of every tree of the garden? (And he spake by the mouth of the serpent.)

"And the woman said unto the serpent: We may eat of the fruit of the trees of the garden; but of the fruit of the tree which thou beholdest in the midst of the garden, God hath said—Ye shall not eat of it, neither shall ye touch it, lest ye die.

"And the serpent said unto the woman: Ye shall not surely die; for God doth know that in the day ye eat thereof, then your eyes shall be opened, and ye shall be as gods, knowing good and evil.

"And when the woman saw that the tree was good for food, and that it became pleasant to the eyes, and a tree to be desired to make her wise, she took of the fruit thereof, and did eat, and also gave unto her husband with her, and he did eat.

"And the eyes of them both were opened, and they knew that they had been naked. And they sewed fig-leaves together and made themselves aprons." (Moses 4:6-13.)

For the protection of the Saints in these latter days, the Lord gave us similar information concerning Satan.

It will be remembered that Joseph Smith and Sidney Rigdon were given a glorious vision of the Savior. It was one of their greatest testimonies:

"And now, after the many testimonies which have been given of him, this is the testimony, last of all, which we give of him: That he lives!

"For we saw him, even on the right hand of God; and we heard the voice bearing record that he is the Only Begotten of the Father—

"That by him, and through him, and of him, the worlds are and were created, and the inhabitants thereof are begotten sons and daughters unto God."

The Prophet continues:

"And this we saw also, and bear record, that an angel of God who was in authority in the presence of God, who rebelled against the Only Begotten Son whom the Father loved and who was in the bosom of the Father, was thrust down from the presence of God and the Son,

"And was called Perdition, for the heavens wept over him—he was Lucifer, a son of the morning.

"And we beheld, and lo, he is fallen! is fallen, even a son of the morning!

"And while we were yet in the Spirit, the Lord commanded us that we should write the vision; for we beheld Satan, that old serpent, even the devil, who rebelled against God, and sought to take the kingdom of our God and his Christ—

"Wherefore, he maketh war with the saints of God, and encompasseth them round about." (D&C 76:22-29.)

The Prophet Joseph was shown more, however; he saw the fate of those who surrender to Satan and join him in his evil way:

"And we saw a vision of the sufferings of those with whom he made war and overcame, for thus came the voice of the Lord unto us:

"Thus saith the Lord concerning all those who know my power, and have been made partakers thereof, and suffered themselves through the power of the devil to be overcome, and to deny the truth and defy my power—

"They are they who are the sons of perdition, of whom I say that it had been better for them never to have been born;

"For they are vessels of wrath, doomed to suffer the wrath of God, with the devil and his angels in eternity;

"Concerning whom I have said there is no forgiveness in this world nor in the world to come—

"Having denied the Holy Spirit after having received

it, and having denied the Only Begotten Son of the Father, having crucified him unto themselves and put him to an open shame.

"These are they who shall go away into the lake of fire and brimstone, with the devil and his angels—

"And the only ones on whom the second death shall have any power;

"Yea, verily, the only ones who shall not be redeemed in the due time of the Lord, after the sufferings of his wrath." (D&C 76:30-38.)

At another time the Lord gave this additional view of the fate of the disobedient: "Wherefore, I, the Lord, have said that the fearful, and the unbelieving, and all liars, and whosoever loveth and maketh a lie, and the whoremonger, and the sorcerer, shall have their part in that lake which burneth with fire and brimstone, which is the second death. Verily I say, that they shall not have part in the first resurrection." (D&C 63:17-18.)

Chapter Thirty-five

HIS VOICE
TO US

Isaiah's voice is one of testimony, and if heeded, it will bring a rich harvest to the faithful.

First and foremost he is a great witness for Christ, telling seven hundred years in advance about Jesus' birth, his ministry in Palestine, and his death.

He identified Jesus as the Holy One of Israel, the Savior, Redeemer, and Messiah, and said that he would be born of a virgin and would be named Immanuel. Jesus was "God with us." But he was also "Wonderful, Counseller, The mighty God, The everlasting Father." (Isaiah 9:6.) Isaiah announced him so.

The humble carpenter of Nazareth was seen by Isaiah as "a man of sorrows, acquainted with grief." His own people disowned him. They hid their faces from him, despised him, and esteemed him not.

All they like sheep had gone astray. As the Holy One of Israel came among them, feeding them by the thousands and healing many of their sick—even raising some of their dead—they nevertheless oppressed him, afflicted him, and brought him as a lamb to the slaughter. As a sheep before her shearers is dumb, so he opened not his mouth.

Yet he bore their iniquities. For their transgressions he was wounded, for their sins he was stricken, but with his stripes they were healed.

He gave his soul as an offering for sin. He made intercession for the transgressors. He died that man might live. All this Isaiah taught.

Jesus was indeed with the wicked in his death, a thief on each side of him. He made his grave with the rich—

but in a borrowed tomb, obtained through the sympathy of Joseph of Arimathea, "an honorable counseller, which also waited for the kingdom of God." (Mark 15:43.) This Joseph was a member of the Jewish Sanhedrin as was Nicodemus, and was regarded as a rich man.

Isaiah foresaw it all.

Jesus brought about the resurrection, and Isaiah declared that all men will be blessed by it. "Thy dead men shall live," he said, "together with my dead body shall they arise." (Isaiah 26:19.) There was no doubt in his mind.

Isaiah gave the first biblical glimpse of salvation for the dead, forecasting the Savior's visit to the realm of the departed, there to pierce the prison doors.

He also would open the eyes of the blind and give hearing to the deaf; and because of his ministry, the meek would increase their joy in the Lord and the poor would rejoice in the Holy One of Israel.

Isaiah's testimony of Christ included enlightening reference to the Lord's latter-day mission: the restoration of the gospel, the rise of Joseph Smith, the publication of the Book of Mormon, the establishment of the Saints in the tops of the mountains, the building of temples, the ultimate gathering of Israel, the second coming of Christ, and the opening of His millennial reign.

What other prophet compares with Isaiah? Was he not great like Moses? Was he not an effective voice crying in the wilderness like John? Is not his message one with tremendous modern significance?

Isaiah! He was a prophet for ancient Judah, it is true, but his message for latter days is magnificent for us.

Isaiah is for today! Great are the words of Isaiah!

INDEX

Abinadi, 41–42
Ahaz, warned by Isaiah, 13–14
"All nations shall flow unto it,"
  56–58, 64–65, 66–70
Amos saw God, 27
Anthon, Charles, 86, 92–97
Ariel, 77–79
Assyrian persuasion, 20–22
Atonement, Isaiah understood,
  30–31
Authorship of book of Isaiah,
  140–42

Balfour treaty, 85
Beesley, Ebenezer, 71
Bible is stick of Judah, 117
Bidamon, Emma Smith, 90–91
Book of Mormon: Isaiah foresaw, 1,
  77–81; helps Latter-day Saints
  understand Isaiah, 5–6, 77–81,
  84–85; predictions about, have
  no meaning to Jews and Gentiles,
  7; translation of, 90–91;
  translated through divine power,
  98–101; is stick of Ephraim,
  115–17

Clark, Rev. John A., 89, 94
Converts, 56–57
Cowdery, Oliver: Savior appears to,
  28; cannot translate, 98–99
Cumorah, 103–4

Dead, salvation of, 48–53
Dead Sea scrolls, 79–80
Destruction of Nephites, 102–8

Dickinson, Ellen E., 89
Disobedient, 158
Douay Bible, 50, 56

Ephraim, gathering of, 114–19
Ezekiel's sticks, 114–19

Gathering of twelve tribes, 114–19
General conferences, 57
Gentile scholars have limited
  understanding, 6–8

Harris, Martin, 86, 92–97, 99, 101
Hezekiah: righteous king, 14–16;
  illness of, 23–25
"High on the Mountain Top," 71–72
Hofmann, Mark William, 93
Howe, Eber D., 89

Isaiah: bore testimony of Christ,
  1–2, 30–33, 43–44, 124; saw God,
  9, 26–29; as political observer, 9;
  family of, 9–10; death of, at
  hands of Manasseh, 10–11; as
  great patriot, 13; advises
  Hezekiah, 14–15; visions of, are
  similar to other prophets; 27–28;
  describes works of Savior, 36;
  and Abinadi, 41–44; affirms
  divinity of Christ, 45–47; first to
  speak of salvation for dead,
  48–53; second chapter of, 54–60;
  sees Salt Lake Temple, 61–63,
  67; made clear by Book of
  Mormon, 77; words of, fulfilled,

108; Jesus quotes, 120–25, 130–131; authorship of, 140–42; as poet, 143–49; teachings of, 150–53; and Lucifer, 154–58; is voice of testimony, 159–160; message of, is for latter days, 160
Isaiah's prophecies on: latter days, 1, 3–4; Savior, 2, 34–40; destruction of Judah, 14; Babylonian captivity, 23–24; atonement, 30–33, 43–44; resurrection, 44; second coming, 44; Book of Mormon, 77–81; gathering of Israel, 132–34

Jerusalem. *See* Old Jerusalem; New Jerusalem
Jerusalem Bible: confirms vision of Isaiah, 29; on salvation of dead, 50; on temple hill, 66–67
Jesus Christ: commands us to study Isaiah, 3; atonement of, 30–33; birth of, 34; retains premortal identity, 35–36; Isaiah confirms divinity of, 45–47; provides salvation for dead, 48–53; quotes Isaiah, 120–25; explains parables, 122; teaches Nephites with words of Isaiah, 126–31; as agent of Father, 127–29; Isaiah taught acceptance of, 150–53
Jews: blind to work of Lord, 5–6; have only secular understanding, 6–9
John quotes Isaiah, 120, 123
John the Baptist identifies himself from words of Isaiah, 120–21
Johnson, Joel H., 71
Judah, invasion of, 13–19

Kirkham, Dr. Francis W., 90–91, 94
Knox translation, 66

Lamanites destroy Nephites, 102–8
Last days, Isaiah prophesies of, 1, 3–4
Latter-day Saints: understand

Isaiah, 5–8; journey of, to Rocky Mountains, foretold by Isaiah, 54–60
Lord Teviot, 64
Lost 116 pages, 99
Lost Tribes, 114, 119, 137–39
Lucifer and Isaiah, 154–58

Manasseh, ordered death of Isaiah, 10–11; born to Hezekiah, 25
Mark quotes Isaiah, 122–23
Masoretic text confirms vision of Isaiah, 28
Matthew quotes Isaiah, 120–22
Mormon, 102–5
Moroni: on Isaiah, 3; buries records 105–7; exhorts readers, 107–8
Moses saw God, 28
"Mountain of the Lord's house," 54–56

Nations "flow" unto temple, 56–57, 64–65, 66–70
Nephi: understood Isaiah, 5; knew Isaiah saw God, 26; used Isaiah as proof of own testimony, 27; explains about sealed book, 82–86; on worth of Book of Mormon, 109, 111–13; speaks of judgments, 110–11
Nephites: destruction of, 102–8; taught by Jesus, 126–31
New English Bible, 50
New Jerusalem, 59–60, 114, 137–38
New World Translation: confirms vision of Isaiah, 29; on temple hill, 67

Obedience, 152–53
Old Jerusalem, war against, 135–39
Ordinances, 73–76
"Other sheep," 127–28
"Out of the dust," 78–80, 85

Paul: referred to Isaiah, 11, 124; on Jesus as agent of Father, 127–28

Peter: testifies of Christ, 42;
identifies prisoners, 49
Poetic ability of Isaiah, 39–40;
143–49
Pratt, Orson, on temple hill, 67–70
Predictions of Isaiah. *See* Isaiah's
prophecies
Prophecies of Isaiah. *See* Isaiah's
prophecies

Repentance, 151
Righteousness taught by Isaiah,
150–53
Rocky Mountains, Saints
established in, 54–58
Roman Catholic Bible, 50, 56

Sabbath, 151–52
Salt Lake Tabernacle, Isaiah saw, 61
Salt Lake Temple: Isaiah saw, in
vision, 61–63; dedication of, 62;
Brigham Young saw, in vision, 63
Satan. *See* Lucifer and Isaiah
Schoenfeld Authentic New
Testament, 49–50
Sealed portion of Book of Mormon,
82–83
Sennacherib, invades Judah, 15–19
Smith, Emma, 90–91
Smith, Joseph: teachings of, provide
background for ancient
prophecies, 6; appearance of
Savior to, 28; given pattern for
temples, 63–64; was unlearned
man, 86–91; translated Book of
Mormon through divine power,
98–101; taught about Satan,
157–58
Smith, Joseph F., vision of, 50–53

Smith, Joseph Fielding, on temples,
54–55
"Sticks" of Judah and Ephraim,
114–19
Symbolism in ordinances, 73–76

Tabernacle. *See* Salt Lake
Tabernacle
Talmage, James E., 75–76
Talmud, death of Isaiah in, 11
Teachings of Isaiah, 150–53
Temple hill, 66–70
Temples, 54–56, 73–76
Three Witnesses, 84–86
Tourists, 56, 64–65
Translation: of general conference
addresses, 57; of Book of
Mormon, 98–101
Trinity in Old Testament, 125
Tucker, Pomeroy, 89

"Unlearned man," 80, 82, 87–91
Urim and Thummim, 99, 100

Widtsoe, John A., 73–76
Wife of Isaiah, 10
Woodruff, Wilford: on Salt Lake
Temple and Tabernacle, 61–62;
prayer of, at dedication of Salt
Lake Temple, 62–63
World Conference on Records,
64–65

Young, Brigham, on Salt Lake
Temple, 63

Zion, 58–60